CICERO

De Amicitia
Selections

CICERO

De Amicitia
Selections

Patsy Rodden Ricks & Sheila K. Dickison

Bolchazy-Carducci Publishers, Inc.
Wauconda, Illinois USA

Contributing Editors
Andrew J. Adams
Laurie Haight Keenan
LeaAnn Osburn

Cover Design
Adam Phillip Velez

Original Illustrations
© 2006 Patricia Lynn Miller

Cicero
De Amicitia Selections

Patsy Rodden Ricks & Sheila K. Dickison

© 2006 Bolchazy-Carducci Publishers, Inc.
All rights reserved.

Bolchazy-Carducci Publishers, Inc.
1000 Brown Street
Wauconda, IL 60084 USA
www.bolchazy.com

Printed in the United States of America
2006
by United Graphics

ISBN-13: 978-0-86516-639-4
ISBN-10: 0-86516-639-0

Library of Congress Cataloging-in-Publication Data

Cicero, Marcus Tullius.
　[Laelius de amicitia. English & Latin. Selections]
　De amicitia : selections / Cicero ; [edited by] Patsy Rodden Ricks & Sheila K. Dickison.
　　p. cm.
　Latin text and English translation; commentary in English.
　Includes bibliographical references.
　ISBN-13: 978-0-86516-639-4 (pbk. : alk. paper)
　ISBN-10: 0-86516-639-0 (pbk. : alk. paper)
　1. Cicero, Marcus Tullius. Laelius de amicitia. 2. Latin language
--Readers. 3. Conduct of life--Early works to 1800. 4. Friendship
--Early works to 1800. I. Ricks, Patsy Rodden. II. Dickison,
Sheila K. (Sheila Kathryn), 1942- . III. Title.
PA6308.L2R53 2006
875'.01--dc22

2006019030

DEDICATION

memoriae parentum: June et Jasper
filiabus optimis: June et Leslie
discipulis meis: "quot sunt quotque fuere, quotque post aliis erunt in annis."

matri carissimae: Nelda Dickison

Contents

Preface

Cicero's *de Amicitia* provides an insight into the relationship of Laelius *sapiens* and Scipio Aemilianus, as well as the subject of friendship as Cicero thought about it based on his readings of the Greek philosophers and his own personal relationships. It was Cicero's lifelong friend Atticus who suggested the topic to him. The modern day reader of Latin is sure to find this work both an example of masterfully written prose and a pleasurable and thought-provoking subject. Cicero's views on friendship are more valuable than ever in this modern world, filled with division and dissension, and they apply to people in general, even though he was defining friendship for his male peers.

We have intended this text not only for AP* and college students, but for high school students in the second or third year who would like to begin their study of Latin authors with Cicero. The aim of the notes in the commentary and the vocabulary is to provide sufficient assistance to students with only a limited background in reading Latin so that the experience may be an enjoyable one. We have chosen to give complete notes even for the sometimes obvious to help the students when working on their own to be successful. Vocabulary help provided has been limited to only those words possible for the context. Stylistic discussions have been limited to the most appropriate examples.

The text for this book has been based on the Gould and Whiteley text with attention given to Powell's suggestions.

The authors would like to thank Patricia Lynn Miller for her exceptional and appropriate drawings. Also we would like to express appreciation to the Latin III students of St. Andrew's Episcopal School, Jackson, Mississippi for readings of and suggestions for the early drafts. We would also like to thank LeaAnn Osborne at Bolchazy-Carducci for her faith that we could produce an appropriate text of the *de Amicitia*. We are extremely thankful to our editors, Andy Adams and the anonymous readers for their helpful suggestions.

---

* AP is a registered trademark of the College Entrance Examination Board, which was not involved in the production of, and does not endorse, this product.

CICERO.
From a bust in the Vatican.

Introduction

A Brief Biography of Cicero's Life

We know more about Marcus Tullius Cicero than any other ancient Roman chiefly due to his voluminous outpouring of writing: his orations, his books on rhetoric, books on philosophical treatises, and his letters, over four hundred of which were written to his lifelong friend Atticus to whom he dedicates the *de Amicitia*.

Cicero was born in 106 BCE near the town of Arpinum. His father, a man of equestrian rank, brought Cicero and his brother Quintus to Rome to be educated. One of Cicero's teachers was the poet Archias, whose citizenship Cicero later defended in 62 BCE. After the Social War of 91–89 BCE, Cicero studied law with Q. Mucius Scaevola, the augur whom Cicero would later use as one of the speakers in the *de Amicitia*. One of Cicero's first orations was his *Pro Roscio Amerino* in which he defended the young Roscius, whose estate had been stolen by Chrysogonus, a favorite of Sulla. Cicero would again challenge Sulla's authority when he prosecuted his political friend Verres in 70 BCE for extortion as governor of Sicily. Cicero's bold daring and his oratorical skills established his reputation in Rome.

Modern-day Arpinum

1

Cicero was proud of the fact that he was elected to all the major offices in the Republic at the earliest age possible and with the most number of votes. In 69 BCE he became aedile, in 66 praetor, and in 63 consul. During his consulship he exposed Catiline as a conspirator, and captured and executed Catiline's followers without holding a trial. Although Rome honored Cicero by giving him the title *pater patriae* for saving the state, Cicero would later suffer for not following the letter of the law.

Publius Clodius, a powerful aristocrat, became Cicero's personal enemy; and in 58 BCE he pushed through a bill that called for the exile of anyone who had executed Roman citizens without a trial. Neither Pompey nor Caesar came to Cicero's aid, and he was forced into exile for 18 months until he was finally recalled in 57. Rejoicing crowds escorted Cicero from Brundisium to Rome, but political power was now in the hands of Pompey and Caesar. The Republic that Cicero loved and defended was past, although he never completely accepted its demise.

After his exile, Cicero devoted his time to writing such works as *de Oratore, de Re Publica, de Legibus*. His last public duty was in 51 BCE when he became governor of Cilicia. In 50 when Cicero returned, he found an Italy on the verge of civil war. Cicero took up Pompey's cause, but was later pardoned by the victorious Julius Caesar.

Cicero's unhappiness caused by Caesar's control of Rome and his own personal problems including divorce and the death of his beloved daughter drove him to a writing frenzy. In two years he wrote such works as *de Finibus, Brutus, Tusculanae Disputationes, de Natura Deorum, de Divinatione, de Senectute, de Amicitia*, and *de Officiis*.

Delighted by Caesar's assassination because he believed the Republic could be restored, Cicero was once again dejected by Antony's push to power. He returned to the public arena to deliver his scathing *Philippics*, a series of stinging speeches against Antony. The passion and daring he had exhibited in prosecuting Verres, in defending Roscius, in challenging Catiline had returned for this last moment of glory in the 63rd and last year of his life. When Antony and Augustus formed the Second Triumvirate, Cicero's fate was sealed. He was proscribed and then killed on December 7, 43 BCE, and his hands and head were nailed to the Rostra where he had known so many successes.

Historical Setting of the
Laelius de Amicitia

Cicero chose the friendship between Scipio Aemilianus and Gaius Laelius to serve as the backdrop for his writings about friendship. Publius Cornelius Scipio Aemilianus Africanus Minor, the son of Lucius Aemilius Paulus and adopted son of Publius Scipio was born about 185 BCE. As a young man, he distinguished himself in the Battle of Pydna in 168, and later during the Third Punic War in 149. By 147 he was the consular commander in Africa and destroyed Carthage. In 134 he was again elected consul in his absence and destroyed Numantia in Spain.

When Scipio returned to Rome, he found the city in turmoil over the reforms of his adopted cousins and brothers-in-law, the Gracchi. Scipio took the side of the Senate, losing much popular support. He died mysteriously at 56 one night after returning home from a fierce debate in the Senate in which he opposed the popular reforms.

Gaius Laelius was the older of the pair by a few years. He was praetor in 145 BCE and consul five years later. He had served with Scipio in Africa and in Spain. Cicero describes him as having *lenitas*, gentleness. He was called *sapiens* for his wisdom.

Scipio and Laelius were part of an intellectual circle that included Roman aristocrats, poets, and learned Greeks such as Polybius, the historian; Panaetius, the philosopher; Terence and Pacuvius, Latin poets; and Lucilius, the satirist.

The Roman Forum in Cicero's Time

THE CHARACTERS IN THE *DE AMICITIA*
A. PARTICIPANTS IN THE DIALOGUE

Gaius Laelius *Sapiens*, son of the elder Laelius, had a distinguished political career achieving the rank of consul in 140 BCE, a notable military career serving under Scipio Aemilianus in Carthage and Numantia, and was perhaps the greatest orator of his day. Due to his love of learning and philosophy he was called "the Wise." He is a great favorite of Cicero who often uses him as an example of a Roman man who is both intellectual and moral. Having been chosen for his erudition and his outstanding friendship with Scipio Aemilianus, Laelius is the persona through whom Cicero speaks in the *de Amicitia.*

Quintus Mucius Scaevola the augur was the son-in-law of Laelius *Sapiens* and the tutor of Cicero in his youth. It is through Scaevola that Cicero had knowledge of Laelius and the younger Scipio.

Gaius Fannius, also Laelius' son-in-law. The role of both Scaevola and Fannius in the *de Amicitia* is to prompt Laelius to speak about the subject of friendship in general from his experience gained through a lifelong friendship with Scipio.

B. P. SCIPIO AEMILIANUS, LAELIUS' DEAR FRIEND
(DISCUSSED IN THE DIALOGUE)

Publius Cornelius Scipio Aemilianus Africanus Minor, the son of Lucius Aemilius Paulus and adopted son of Publius Scipio (son of Scipio Africanus). After his defeat of Carthage in the Third Punic War, he was given the surname of Africanus to which the name Minor was attached to distinguish him from his adopted grandfather, Scipio Africanus Maior. He and Laelius *Sapiens* were the chief members of a literary circle that included Terence, the famous Roman comedy playwright. Scipio Aemilianus died suddenly in his home after a day of fierce debate in the Senate in which Scipio stood firm in his views against the popular reforms pushed forward by Tiberius and Gaius Gracchus. Cicero and many others believed Scipio was murdered. The time period of the *de Amicitia* is only a few days after Scipio's death.

Tree of the Scipio and Laelius Family Members Central to de Amicitia

Scipio Family

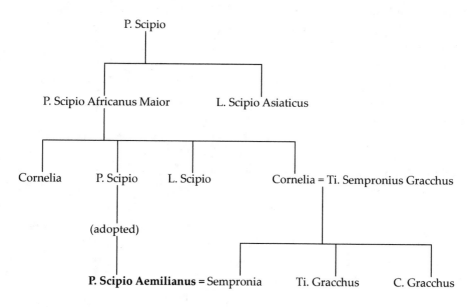

P. Scipio

P. Scipio Africanus Maior   L. Scipio Asiaticus

Cornelia   P. Scipio   L. Scipio   Cornelia = Ti. Sempronius Gracchus

(adopted)

P. Scipio Aemilianus = Sempronia   Ti. Gracchus   C. Gracchus

Laelius Family

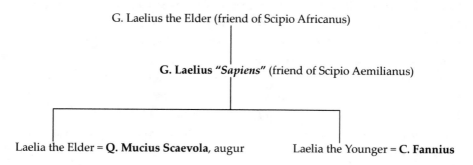

G. Laelius the Elder (friend of Scipio Africanus)

G. Laelius "*Sapiens*" (friend of Scipio Aemilianus)

Laelia the Elder = **Q. Mucius Scaevola**, augur   Laelia the Younger = **C. Fannius**

Summary of Sections I.1–IV.16
of DE AMICITIA

[1–5] In the introduction to the *de Amicitia*, Cicero tells us that Atticus, surely his closest friend, suggested to him the idea of writing about friendship. Enthusiastic about the subject, Cicero proposes to use Laelius Sapiens as his speaker in this new work just as he had previously used Cato to speak for Cicero himself on the subject of old age in his *Cato, de Senectute*. The purpose of these personae, as he states, is that thus he will not have to interject the pronoun "I" into his narrative and that the use of men famous in earlier times as authorities on their subjects will lend more weight to the discussion.

Cicero chooses Laelius as his speaker because of his long-lasting and close friendship with Scipio Aemilianus, and because this friendship was well known in Cicero's day. Cicero's knowledge of these matters, as he tells his reader, is through his apprenticeship with Quintus Mucius Scaevola, the augur who was the young Cicero's instructor. Scaevola, the son-in-law of Laelius, was privy to the accounts of Laelius and Scipio's friendship because Laelius was accustomed to discuss his relationship with Scipio with his two sons-in-law, Scaevola and Gaius Fannius. At least Cicero so alleges, in order to provide a note of authenticity to his version of the conversation.

[6–9] The *de Amicitia* begins in mid-conversation between Laelius and his sons-in-law as they contemplate the recent death of Scipio. Fannius states that men in Rome call Laelius *sapiens* (wise) because of his character and nature but also for his learning and intellectual abilities. He mentions that many before have called Cato wise and all have called Socrates wise as the oracle of Apollo named him *sapientissum* (most wise of men). But it is Laelius that Romans think wise, because he is able to judge matters in his own mind and to believe that all human misfortunes may be overcome with virtue. Fannius and Scaevola have suggested that Laelius' absence from the recent meeting of the augurs was due to illness and not his recent bereavement at the death of Scipio because they believe in Laelius' stoic nature and his ability to control his grief.

Laelius affirms his sons-in-law's belief that grief would not keep him away from his duties. He accepts Fannius' compliment in calling him *sapiens*, but states his opinion that Cato was especially so and that Cato was very admirable in his ability to accept his own son's death. Laelius then begins to explain his feeling about his friend Scipio and his death.

[10–15] Laelius affirms that Scipio was the best friend he ever had, but affirms that he has means to console himself after the loss of Scipio. Rather than believing that Scipio's death is a tragic event, he believes that whatever bad has happened grieves him personally, but to pity himself would be selfish.

Laelius gives a brief review of Scipio's life: he was made consul twice even though he did not run for the office; he destroyed both Carthage and Numantia, thus putting an end to present and future hostilities. He had an easy manner and was dutiful to his mother, sisters, household, and to mankind in general; he was popular at Rome. What more could this man have gained, asks Laelius, if he had lived longer? At least he was spared the weakness of old age. Laelius recounts that the best day of Scipio's life was the day before he died, when he was escorted home from the Senate after opposing the popular party. (Scipio's death that very night was not without suspicion of murder.)

The fact that Laelius believes in the immortality of the soul helps him to think that Scipio is now with the gods; but he adds that if he is incorrect and there is no immortality, then there is also no pain to the deceased and only joy in the remembrance of the friend for those left behind.

Laelius believes that he is less fortunate and should have died first, being the older of the two. He recounts that his friendship with Scipio was shared in both public and private matters, and Laelius hopes to be remembered more for sharing one of the truly deep friendships than for being called *sapiens*, a title he feels he does not deserve.

[16–17] On being asked by Scaevola and Fannius to discuss the nature and boundaries of friendship as he has discussed other subjects in the past, Laelius at first is hesitant because he feels someone better schooled in Greek philosophy might present a more learned discussion, but he is willing enough to communicate what he has learned through a lifelong friendship with Scipio.

Latin Text of *de Amicitia* with Commentary

HELP WITH USING THE COMMENTARY

A&G = *Allen and Greenough's New Latin Grammar* (Ginn & Company: New York, 1931). Grammatical points may also be checked in any other comprehensive grammar.

< = is from

A Latin word or phrase in parentheses indicates that the Latin is understood or implied from context.

When two translations are given, the first translation is literal, the second closer to acceptable English.

ABBREVIATIONS USED IN THE COMMENTARY

adv. = adverb
m. = masculine
f. = feminine
n. = neuter
pl. = plural
conj. = conjunction
adj. = adjective
SMALL CAPS = a term found in the glossary of Figures of Speech
† = required on Advanced Placement exams

NUMBERING SYSTEM

Numbers in the commentary are listed by line numbers assigned for ease of reading in this text. The standard roman numerals and arabic numbers designating sections and subsections are given in brackets, both in the Latin text and in the commentary, as they occur. These are standard numerations for *de Amicitia* and allow for easy cross-reference to other texts.

Selection A: Lines 1–107 [Sections V.17–VII.23]
Part 1: lines 1–28

After urging his sons-in-law to put friendship before everything else, Laelius states that friendship cannot exist except between "good" men. Laelius then considers the difference between the philosophers' definition of "good men" and the everyday definition.

1.   [V. 17] **tantum**, adv.: only.

2.   **anteponatis**: takes an accusative with the direct object (**amicitiam**) and a dative (**omnibus rebus humanis**) as a compound verb. The verb is subjunctive in an indirect command after **hortari**.

2–3.   Note Cicero's parallel constructions: **tam . . . aptum, tam conveniens** (†anaphora), **vel secundas vel adversas,** and his use of †asyndeton here.

3.   **aptum** < **aptus, -a, -um**: suitable, suited; takes the dative case (**naturae**).

     conveniens, -venientis: adapted to, suited to; takes **ad** with the accusative. [The reader should think about why **amicitia** would be suited to both good times and bad.]

4.   **secundas** < **secundus, -a, -um**: favorable.

5.   [18] **hoc**: "this thing"; less literally, "this principle"; accusative, object of **sentio**.

     primum: adv.

5–6.   **nisi . . . amicitiam . . . esse non posse**: "that friendship can not exist except . . ." Translate as in apposition to the **hoc** above: "I understand this principle (namely) that friendship is not able to exist except . . ."

     [In the course of his discussion, Laelius refers several times to the belief of certain philosophers that only "good men" have the ability to maintain "good" relationships such as friendship.]

5.   **bonis** < **boni, bonorum**, m. pl.: good men.

6–7.   **neque id ad vivum reseco**: "nor am I pruning that thing (the definition) back to the quick"; (less literally) "I do not (want to) prune the definition back to the quick."

     Cicero uses figurative language here (the imagery of pruning a shrub or a fingernail back to its living core or quick) to suggest that he does not wish to delve deeply into these matters, splitting hairs in arguments, as the Stoics do.

     Cicero may also be suggesting with this choice of imagery that if he adopted the idea of the philosophers who believe that only "good men" can have friendships, then there would be few if any friendships; therefore, he would be "cutting to the heart" of friendships by denying their existence among ordinary men who could never fit the philosopher's esoteric definition of "good."

6.   **id**: accusative, direct object of **reseco**. **Id** refers to the idea that there are no good men; therefore no friendships.

7.   <u>ut</u> **. . . disserunt**: "as . . . ," a parenthetical clause.

ab   **illi qui haec subtilius disserunt**: Laelius has in mind the Stoics who split hairs in their discussions.

     subtilius < **subtiliter**: precisely, exactly, accurately, in too much detail; comparative adv.

     disserunt < **dissero, dissere, disserui, dissertum**: discuss, argue.

[V. 17] *Laelius.* Ego vos hortari <u>tantum</u> possum ut amicitiam omnibus rebus humanis <u>anteponatis</u>; nihil est enim <u>tam</u> naturae <u>aptum</u>, <u>tam</u> <u>conveniens</u> ad res vel <u>secundas</u> vel adversas.

5   **[18]** Sed <u>hoc</u> <u>primum</u> sentio <u>nisi</u> in <u>bonis</u> amici-tiam <u>esse</u> <u>non</u> <u>posse</u>; <u>neque</u> <u>id</u> <u>ad</u> <u>vivum</u> re-<u>seco</u>, <u>ut</u> illi qui haec <u>subtilius</u> <u>disserunt</u>, fortasse

8. **vere**, adv.: accurately, truthfully.

   ad communem utilitatem: "to everyday interest; for ordinary usefulness"; i.e., the difference between a philosopher's discussion of friendship to a learned audience in which the topic is abstract and an ordinary person's discussion in a true group of friends. (Laelius does not intend to argue about who may be a good man, splitting hairs over the definition, but does intend to provide a common sense definition.)

   parum, adv.: little, not enough, not sufficiently.

9. **quemquam . . . virum bonum esse**: accusative and infinitive dependent on **negant** in indirect statement.

10. **sit ita**: "let it be so, granted it is so." **Sit** is present jussive subjunctive. Note the †ALLITERATION of *s* here.

    sane: certainly, by all means.

    eam: demonstrative adjective, modifying **sapientiam**.

    interpretantur < interpretor, interpretari, interpretatus sum: explain, understand, call.

11. **quam**: relative pronoun; antecedent is **eam sapientiam**.

    adhuc: yet, still.

    mortalis: in apposition to **nemo** ("no one, a mortal that is").

    est consecutus < consequor, consequi, consecutus sum: reach, attain.

8–13. The Stoics believed that the **vir sapiens** was an ideal that could not be attained by mortals although they allowed that a few men such as Socrates had come close to the ideal.

13. **ea**: accusative. pl. neuter, direct object of **spectare**.

    finguntur < fingo, fingere, finxi, fictum: imagine, invent, devise.

14. **dicam**: potential subjunctive; "I would say."

14–15. Gaius Fabricius Luscinus, Manius Curius Dentatus, and Tiberius Coruncanius were all heroes of the Roman Republic who were known for their honesty, leadership, and duty to the state. They served as examples of men who lived honest and good lives.

    C. Fabricium . . . fuisse sapientes: accusative and infinitive dependent on **dicam** in indirect statement.

15. **maiores, maiorum**, m. pl.: ancestors.

16. **ad istorum normam**: "to their (the Stoic) measure." **Norma** is a carpenter's square. Laelius continues to believe that men can be good even if not perfectly good, but allows that the Stoics would not consider these Romans so even allowing for their virtues.

17. **sibi . . . habeant**: jussive subjunctive. ("Let them keep for themselves").

17–18. **et invidiosum et obscurum**: "both unacceptable and incomprehensible."

18. **concedant**: jussive subjunctive. ("Let them grant").

    ut . . . fuerint: substantive clause of purpose after **concedo** (verbs of permitting and granting may be followed by a subjunctive clause beginning with **ut**); translate as "grant that . . ." **boni viri** is the predicate nominative after **fuerint**.

18–19. **ne . . . quidem**: not even.

18–19. **Ne id . . . facient; negabunt . . . id**: note Cicero's use of †ASYNDETON between the two verbs in †CHIASTIC order.

19. **id . . . posse**: indirect statement after **negabunt**; **id** stands for the term "good."

    sapienti: to a wise man; "they will deny that that (name) 'good' can be granted except to a wise man." The Stoics cling to their ideal that only the truly wise man can be good.

vere, sed ad communem utilitatem parum; negant
enim quemquam virum bonum esse nisi sapientem.

10   Sit ita sane; sed eam sapientiam interpretantur
quam adhuc mortalis nemo est consecutus. [Nos
autem ea quae sunt in usu vitaque communi, non
ea quae finguntur aut optantur, spectare debemus.
Nunquam ego dicam C. Fabricium, M'. Curium, Ti.

15   Coruncanium, quos sapientes nostri maiores iudi-
cabant, ad istorum normam fuisse sapientes. Qua
re sibi habeant sapientiae nomen et invidiosum et
obscurum; concedant ut hi boni viri fuerint. Ne
id quidem facient; negabunt id nisi sapienti posse

19–20.   **[19] agamus**: hortatory subjunctive, "let us continue on, let us keep going."

pingui Minerva: ablative of respect (in accordance with) [A&G 418 a] or perhaps descriptive ablative [A&G 415]. This is an example of †METONYMY: the substitution of Minerva for the head or the thinking process as Minerva was the goddess of wisdom; **pingui Minerva** would mean "with our own dull wit"; or "with our own lack of intellect"; **ut aiunt**, "as they say," introduces a proverbial Latin expression.

20–28.   In this section Laelius moves away from Stoic philosophical quibbling to state that he believes that men who act according to the principles he describes in 21–28 must, from a practical standpoint, be called "good."

Before the grammatical commentary, we provide a literal translation for this difficult sentence (**Qui . . . ducem**): "(Those) who so conduct themselves, so live that their honesty, integrity, fairness, generosity is proven, nor that there is in them any greed, lust, recklessness and that they are men of great strength of character, as those men were whom I named just now, let us consider that these men ought to be called good men, as they are considered, because they follow, as much as men can, nature as the best guide for living well."

Shuckburgh (p. 6, www.fordham.edu/halsall/ancient/cicero-friendship-html) translates less literally: "We mean then by the "good" those whose actions and lives leave no question as to their honor, purity, equity, and liberality; who are free from greed, lust, and violence; and who have the courage of their convictions. Those men I have just named may serve as examples. Such men as these being generally accounted "good," let us agree to call them so, on the ground that to the best of human ability they follow nature as the most perfect guide to a good life."

Note that in this translation Cicero's one long and highly elaborate sentence is broken down into *three* sentences in English! Cicero's achieves this subordination with two parallel relative clauses, four result clauses, an indicative subordinate clause, another relative clause, a second indicative subordinate clause, a passive periphrastic in an accusative and infinitive construction, and finally a subordinate adverbial clause (begins with **quia**) with a subordinate clause inside it (begins with **quantum**).

21.   **qui**: those who.

se gerunt: conduct themselves.

eorum: "their"; possessive referring to **qui** and modifying the qualities of **fides** and **liberalitas** in the next line.

21–22.   **ut . . . probetur**: subjunctive in a result clause after **ita . . . gerunt, ita vivunt**.

22.   **fides, integritas, aequitas, liberalitas**: each is considered as the singular subject of **probetur**.

aequitas: fairness; reasonableness.

liberalitas: generosity.

22–23.   **nec sit . . . sintque**: also result clauses with **ita** in line 21. Since this sentence is so long, it is likely the reader will not remember what the construction was at the beginning. Rather than translating literally, switch to the indicative: "and that there is not in these men any greed, lust (and) daring and that they are of great strength of character . . ."

24.   **magna constantia**: great strength of character; ablative of description.

modo: just now.

ut ei fuerunt: ut + indicative = as.

20   concedi. **[19]** Agamus igitur pingui Minerva, ut
aiunt. Qui ita se gerunt, ita vivunt, ut eorum
probetur fides, integritas, aequitas, liberalitas, nec
sit in eis ulla cupiditas, libido, audacia, sintque
magna constantia, ut ei fuerunt modo quos

Abl or descriptn.

Ut + Ind = as or When

24–25.   **ut ei . . . nominavi**: these clauses refer back to the list of names Cicero made above of those whom the past considered **boni viri**.

25.   **hos viros bonos**: an appositive with **quos** in line 24, "as those were whom just now I have named, those good men."

ut habiti sunt: "as they have been considered."

25–26.   **hos viros . . . putemus**: translate in this order: **putemus hos viros bonos (ut habiti sunt) sic etiam appellandos [esse]. putemus**, the main verb of the sentence, is a hortatory subjunctive which sets up the indirect statement (**hos viros bonos appellandos [esse]**). The infinitive that serves as the verb (**appellandos [esse]**) is also a passive periphrastic.

26.   **sequantur**: subjunctive in an explanatory clause introduced by **quia** following an indirect statement (**appellandos [esse]**); the subjunctive indicates that the subordinate clause expresses the thought of someone other than the writer or speaker.

quantum: subordinate conj.; as much; in as far as.

27–28.   **optimam . . . ducem** is in apposition to **naturam; ducem**, although usually a masculine noun, is feminine here because it stands in apposition to the feminine noun, **natura**.

According to the Stoic point of view **natura** as it is used here represents the Stoic idea of **summum bonum** (the highest good).

POINTS TO PONDER:

In the Stoic position, only the sapiens or philosopher/wise man is "good." Laelius' opinion is that men who have generally been accepted as "good" should be considered so.

Is Laelius' opinion valid?

25　nominavi, hos viros bonos, ut habiti sunt, sic etiam appellandos putemus, quia sequantur quantum homines possunt naturam optimam bene vivendi ducem.

PART 2: LINES 29–43

Natural relationships, such as citizenship in the same country, join men together, but friendship is stronger than these natural ties.

29–43. The argument in this paragraph is somewhat difficult to grasp; below is a summary.

There are certain bonds of friendship among all men, but the bonds are greater among men whose ties are greater; therefore, men of the same country feel stronger bonds toward each other than towards men of other countries, and men feel stronger bonds toward their relatives than they do toward fellow citizens with whom they do not share family ties. Although friendships between fellow citizens and relatives exist, these friendships are not as strong as the friendship between two or a few men who are united by goodwill. The point seems to be that casual friendships can exist among men who have common bonds but intense friendships can only exist among very small numbers of men.

29. **mihi perspicere videor**: "I seem to myself to understand"; (less literally) "it seems clear to me."

29–30. **natos esse nos**: indirect statement dependent on **perspicere**. **Nos** is the subject of the accusative and infinitive construction.

30. **ut . . . esset**: subjunctive in a result clause after **ita**.

societas, societatis, f.: tie, connection.

maior: modifies **societas**; the idea is that the more we have in common, the greater are our ties.

"INTER OMNES ESSET SOCIETAS QUAEDAM"

31. **ut . . . accederet**: verb is subjunctive because it is a subordinate clause in indirect statement. Translate "as each person approaches most closely (to us.)" Verb in the **ut** clause is in secondary sequence because of the tense of **natos esse** (see A&G 485 j: "when a clause depends on one already dependent, its sequence may be secondary if the verb of that clause expresses past time, even if the main verb is primary tense.")

30   Sic enim mihi perspicere videor, ita natos esse
nos ut inter omnes esset societas quaedam, maior
autem, ut quisque proxime accederet. Itaque cives

32. **potiores quam**: "preferable to" (literally "more powerful than"). Supply *sunt* as the verb in the sentence.

    peregrini < peregrinus, -i, m.: foreigner, stranger.

    propinqui < propinquus, -i, m.: relative, kinsman. Supply *potiores*.

    alieni < alienus, -i, m.: a stranger; i.e., someone not related to you by birth.

33. **his**: refers back to **cives** and **propinqui**.

    peperit < pario, parere, peperi, partum: give birth to, produce, create.

34. **ea**: refers back to **amicitia**.

    firmitatis < firmitas, firmitatis, f.: constancy, steadfastness, strength. Here partitive genitive with **satis** ("enough (of) strength, sufficient strength").

    hoc: "in this respect" (ablative of respect).

    praestat: takes a dative (**propinquitati**).

35. **propinquitati < propinquitas, propinquitatis**, f.: kinship, relationship by birth.

36. **tolli < tollo, tollere, sustuli, sublatum**: eliminate, remove, destroy (present passive infinitive).

    non potest: supply *tolli*. Latin does not use a contrasting conjunction between the clauses **quod ex . . . potest** and **ex amicitia non potest**; supply a "but" between these two clauses in your English translation.

36–37. **sublata . . . benevolentia**: ablative absolute; translate this Latin construction as a conditional clause ("if . . . ").

    benevolentia: affection, kindness.

    In the *de Amicitia* one of Laelius' (and thus Cicero's) main points is that friendship cannot exist without **benevolentia** (goodwill, kindness, affection).

38. **propinquitatis**: supply *nomen*.

38–43. **[20]** This sentence states that there are many kinds of connections between human beings, but friendship is special because the connections are so tight and affection is shared only among a very few men.

38. **quanta**: how great, as great; modifies **vis**.

    quanta . . . sit: an indirect question dependent on **intellegi**.

40. **conciliavit < concilio, conciliare, conciliavi, conciliatum**: form, unite, bring about.

41. **res**: stands here for **amicitia**.

41–42. **adducta (est) in angustum**: reduced in measure, narrowed.

42–43. **ut . . . iungeretur**: result clause. Translate as present tense. "A general truth after a past tense follows the sequence of tenses." (A&G 485 d)

42. **caritas, caritatis**, f.: regard; love, affection.

POINTS TO PONDER:

How does Laelius prove his argument that friendship is stronger than other natural bonds?

Among the hierarchy of relationships where is the bond of affection strongest?

potiores quam peregrini, propinqui quam alieni:
cum his enim amicitiam natura ipsa peperit, sed
ea non satis habet firmitatis] Namque hoc praestat
35   amicitia propinquitati quod ex propinquitate benevolentia tolli potest, ex amicitia non potest: sublata enim benevolentia amicitiae nomen tollitur,
propinquitatis manet. **[20]** Quanta autem ⎡vis⎤
amicitiae sit ⎡ex hoc intellegi maxime potest, quod
40   ex infinita societate generis humani, quam conciliavit ipsa natura, ita contracta res est et adducta in
angustum ut omnis caritas aut inter duos aut inter
paucos iungeretur.

PART 3: LINES 44–65

Laelius gives a general list of desires and pleasures that men praise. Friendship and goodness are the highest in his opinion.

44–64.   [VI.] Laelius offers a definition of friendship and then compares friendship with other ideals on which men place importance in life such as good will, wisdom, riches, wealth, power, pleasure, and virtue.

44–45.   **omnium divinarum humanarumque rerum**: an objective genitive dependent on **consensio**; translate here as "harmony of . . . , agreement on . . . "

45.   **cum**: joined with.

46.   **consensio, consensionis**, f.: an agreement, harmony.

46–47.   **qua . . . an**: literally "than which in fact I do not know whether." **qua**: ablative of comparison referring to **amicitia** and dependent on **melius; qua** serves as a connecting relative and should be translated less literally as "this," referring back to **amicitia**. Translate: "I do not know in fact whether anything better than this (friendship) . . . "

46–48.   Construe the sentence as: **haud scio an . . . nil . . . melius . . . sit . . . datum.**

47.   **excepta sapientia**: ablative absolute; **excepta < excipio**.

48.   **sit . . . datum**: take **nil** as the subject. Verb is subjunctive in an indirect question dependent on **haud scio an**.

    divitias < divitiae, -arum, f.: riches.

49.   **valetudinem < valetudo, valetudinis**, f.: health.

50.   **voluptates < voluptas, voluptatis**, f.: pleasure; sexual pleasure.

48–50.   Note the artistic word order Cicero uses to make his case ultimately that some men make poor choices in not preferring virtue and friendship.

50.   **beluarum < belua, beluae**, f.: beast; animal. Genitive of characteristic (A&G 343 c); take in the predicate after (*est*) (". . . is [characteristic] of brute beasts").

50–51.   **beluarum . . . extremum**: supply *est*.

51.   **extremum**: refers back to **voluptates** ("this last thing").

    illa . . . superiora, n. pl.: refers to all the desires mentioned above.

    caduca < caducus, -a, -um: frail, transitory, perishable. Supply *sunt*.

52.   **posita** < perfect passive participle of **pono**, here modifying **illa**. With **in** + the ablative means "dependent on."

    tam . . . quam: so . . . as.

53.   **temeritate < temeritas, temeritatis**, f.: whim; caprice.

    qui = ei qui: "those who."

    Throughout *de Amicitia* Laelius insists that friendship depends entirely on the concept of **virtus** (goodness, moral worth, moral perfection, virtue) without which friendship cannot exist.

54.   **praeclare illi quidem**: use the order "illi quidem (plural verb understood) praeclare." English would supply a verb like "do so" for the understood verb of the Latin. Note **quidem** follows the word it emphasizes. Translate: "Those who, however, place the highest good in virtue, those men in fact do so nobly."

    praeclare: especially well, nobly, very well.

55.   **gignit < gigno, gignere, genui, genitum**: give birth to, produce.

    continet: here translate as "sustains, preserves."

[VI.] Est autem amicitia nihil aliud nisi omnium
45   divinarum humanarumque rerum cum benevolentia et caritate consensio; qua quidem haud scio
an excepta sapientia nil unquam melius homini
sit a dis immortalibus datum. Divitias alii prae-
ponunt, bonam alii valetudinem, alii potentiam,
50   alii honores, multi etiam voluptates. Beluarum hoc
quidem extremum; illa autem superiora caduca et
incerta, posita non tam in consiliis nostris quam
in fortunae temeritate. [Qui autem in virtute summum bonum ponunt,] praeclare illi quidem, sed
55   haec ipsa virtus amicitiam et gignit et continet,

56. **ullo pacto**: ablative of respect ("in any manner, at all").

58. **[21] interpretemur** like **metiamur** (line 59), **numeremus** (line 60), **omittamus** (line 62) are hortatory subjunctives.

58. **eam** stands for **virtutem < virtus**, f., accusative object of **metiamur**.

59. **magnificentia**: ablative.

60. **qui habentur**: translate literally as "who are (so) considered; who are considered (good)." Cicero again emphasizes that he is using a commonsense definition of "**boni viri**" (refer to lines 20–28 above where he made this point emphatically)—not the Stoic definition that is the ideal and nobody meets.

STATUE OF CICERO AT ARPINUM

nec sine virtute amicitia esse ullo pacto potest. [21] Iam virtutem ex consuetudine vitae sermonisque nostri interpretemur, nec eam, ut quidam docti, verborum magnificentia metiamur,

60   virosque bonos eos qui habentur numeremus,

61.   **Paulos, Catones, Gallos, Scipiones, Philos**: take in apposition to **viros bonos**. Laelius mentions these men in the plural to stand for all men who exhibit the same strength of character as was found among them. Lucius Aemilius Paulus was a great general and the father of Scipio Aemilianus; Marcus Porcius Cato was known for his integrity and severity; Gaius Sulpicius Gallus was consul and a famous orator; Lucius Furius Philus was a friend of Laelius and the Scipios; Scipio Aemilianus was Laelius' dearest friend.

61–62.   **his communis vita contenta est**: ordinary life is satisfied with these (men); i.e., these men satisfy the ordinary standard for "good men"; **contenta**: takes ablative.

63.   **omnino**: "at all" with the negative. Cicero again refers to the perfect men Stoic philosophy describes. Cicero does not believe these men exist in reality.

   tales: modifies **viros**.

64.   **tantas . . . quantas**: correlatives; "such great opportunities . . . as."

   habet: here means "offers."

65.   **queo, quire, quivi (quii), quitum**: be able; can.

   dicere < dico, dicere, dixi, dictum: explain; describe.

Points to Ponder:

What is the *"consensio"* in line 46 that brings people into the bond of friendship?

What are the priorities valued by some people that Laelius says depend on the rashness of fortune?

According to Laelius, how does one interpret *virtus*?

Paulos, Catones, Gallos, Scipiones, Philos: his communis vita contenta est: eos autem omittamus qui
omnino nusquam reperiuntur. Tales igitur inter
viros amicitia tantas opportunitates habet quantas
65   vix queo dicere.

PART 4: LINES 66–87

Beginning with line 66, Cicero makes the case for the pleasures and advantages that friendship brings.

66.   **[22] principio**, adv.: in the first place.

      qui: archaic ablative used as an adv. meaning "how."

      vitalis: "worth living"; nominative completion of **esse**. ("How can life be worth living?")

67.   **Ennius,** whom the Romans regarded as the father of Latin poetry, was born in 239 BCE. He wrote tragedies and the *Annales*, a history of Rome from its mythical beginnings to his own time. Although only fragments of his works now remain, Roman writers such as Cicero who frequently refers to him as "our own dear Ennius" often quote from his works. Cato the Elder brought him to Rome, and when he died in his seventies, he was buried in the Scipio family tomb.

67–68.   **quae . . . conquiescat**: subjunctive in a relative clause of characteristic ("of the kind which does not rest . . . ").

      conquiescat: Powell reads as **conquiescit**. The use of an indicative seems to be a better reading as then the relative **quae** refers to an antecedent (**vita vitalis**) that is concrete and definite.

67.   **amici**: genitive singular dependent on **benevolentia**.

68.   **quid dulcius**: supply *est*.

      quicum: archaic form of **quocum**; translate "(someone) with whom."

69.   **audeas**: subjunctive in a relative clause of characteristic ("with whom you would dare . . . ").

69–73.   In the following two sentences Cicero uses contrary to fact conditions to make his case by asking what it would be like not to have a friend in certain circumstances. This is an emphatic way of stating that one needs a close friend to make prosperity more enjoyable, just as one needs such a friend to help bear adverse situations.

69.   **qui**: translate here as "how"; archaic ablative used as an adv.

69–70.   **esset . . . nisi haberes**: imperfect subjunctives in a contrary to fact condition. ("How would there be such great enjoyment in prosperous times, unless you were to have [someone] who might rejoice equally in them (your good times) as you yourself [do]?")

70.   **qui**: relative pronoun; supply (someone) as the antecedent (A&G 307 c).

      illis: dative with **gauderet; illis** refers to **prosperis rebus**.

71.   **tu ipse:** *gauderes* is understood here.

      aeque ac: equally, as much . . . as.

      adversas: supply *res*.

72.   **difficile esset**: "it would be difficult." Understand the two subjunctive verbs (**esset** and **ferret**) as an implied contrary to fact condition, expressing a position similar to that of the previous sentence. (The thought is that it be would difficult to bear adverse circumstances if one did not have someone who bore these circumstances more strenuously than one did oneself. When one has a true friend, an alter ego, the implication is that it is not difficult to bear adversity.)

72.   **illas**: refers to **adversas**.

      gravius: comparative adv.

73.   **tu:** *ferres* is understood here.

      expetuntur < expeto, expetere, expetivi, expetitum: desire.

[22] Principio, qui potest esse vita vitalis, ut ait Ennius, quae non in amici mutua benevolentia conquiescat? Quid dulcius quam habere quicum omnia audeas sic loqui ut tecum? Qui esset tantus

70 fructus in prosperis rebus, nisi haberes qui illis aeque ac tu ipse gauderet? Adversas vero ferre difficile esset sine eo qui illas gravius etiam quam tu ferret. Denique ceterae res quae expetuntur

F.

74. **opportunae sunt singulae rebus fere singulis**: "are individually suited for the most part to individual matters"; i.e., men have certain desires for specific reasons. Latin uses an adjective here (**singulae**) where English uses an adv. The **rebus** refers to the nouns listed below: **divitiae . . . opes . . . honores . . . voluptates . . . valetudo.**

rebus . . . singulis: dative with **opportunae.**

fere: adv.

75–76. **utare . . . colare . . . laudere**: the alternative form for the 2nd singular subjunctive passive used in purpose clauses introduced by **ut**. [Note that **utare** is a deponent verb; the more common forms are **utaris . . . colaris . . . lauderis.**]

75. **opes < ops, opis**, f.: power.

colare < colo, colere, colui, cultum: honor, esteem.

76. **dolore**: ablative with **careas.**

77. **muneribus**: ablative with **fungare.**

fungare: the alternative form for the 2nd singular deponent subjunctive of **fungor.**

78. **continet**: embraces.

quoquo: wherever, adv. functioning as a conjunction.

verteris: future perfect tense. Latin emphasizes that this action will have taken place before the time of the main verb. **Te** is the reflexive object of **verteris.**

praesto, adv.: ready at hand, present.

79–80. **est . . . excluditur . . . est**: understand *amicitia* as the subject of these three verbs.

Note that the verbs **est . . . excluditur . . . est** provide an example of †ASYNDETON, a stylistic device that emphasizes the point that friendship is ubiquitous. Also note the use of †ANAPHORA in **nullo . . . nunquam . . . nunquam.**

79. **nullo loco** is an ablative of separation with **excluditur.**

intempestivus, -a, -um: out of season (adj.).

80–81. **non aqua, non igni, ut aiunt**: fire and water were considered two essentials for life and therefore proverbial ("as they say"). A court sentence that forbid someone from the use of fire and water (**aqua et igni interdicere**) was a death sentence. **non aqua, non igni**: repetition of the negative with these proverbial nouns, rather than the verb, makes the point forcefully that friendship is of universal use.

aqua . . . igni . . . amicitia: ablatives dependent on **utimur.**

81. **locis pluribus**: supply *in.*

82–84. **vulgari, mediocri, vera, perfecta**: all modify the understood noun *amicitia.*

83. **prodest < prosum, prodesse, profui**: benefit; takes the dative.

opportunae sunt singulae rebus fere singulis;
75   divitiae ut utare; opes ut colare; honores ut laudere; voluptates ut gaudeas; valetudo ut dolore
careas et muneribus fungare corporis: amicitia
res plurimas continet. Quoquo te verteris praesto
est: nullo loco excluditur: nunquam intempestiva,
80   nunquam molesta est. Itaque non aqua, non igni,
ut aiunt, locis pluribus utimur quam amicitia.
Neque ego nunc de vulgari aut de mediocri, quae
tamen ipsa et delectat et prodest, sed de vera et

84.   **qualis**: refers to **amicitia**.

84–85.   **qualis . . . fuit:** *talis* is understood in this sentence as being correlative to **qualis;**
  talis . . . qualis, such . . . as; "(such friendship) as that of those was who a few are
  named"; translate less literally "such as was the friendship of those few who are
  mentioned." **Pauci** is incorporated into the relative clause when one might expect from
  English that it would be a genitive antecedent of **qui**.

85–87.   **splendidiores . . . leviores:** note the parallel construction in the two halves of this
  sentence (**facit secundas res splendidiores . . . [facit] adversas [res] leviores**).

86.   **partiens** < **partior** (and **partio, partire, partivi, partitum**): divide.

  communicans < **communico, communicare, communicavi, communicatum**: share.

  partiens communicansque: present active participles modifying **amicitia**. Cicero here
  enunciates a lovely thought about the value of friendship: it doubles pleasures but
  relieves troubles by dividing them in half.

POINTS TO PONDER:

What specifically are the benefits of friendship mentioned by Laelius?

Define the following words and give their benefits according to the text:
divitiae, opes, honores, voluptates, valetudo.

Explain what Laelius means when he says: *non aqua, non igni . . . locis pluribus
utimur quam amicitia.*

perfecta loquor, qualis eorum qui pauci nominantur
85   fuit. Nam et secundas res splendidiores facit
amicitia, et adversas partiens communicansque
leviores.

Part 5: lines 88–107

Laelius discusses the practical benefits of friendship and the effect on the world if friendship did not exist. He suggests that the main benefit is hope for the future and strength for the spirit. Since he experienced such a deep friendship with Scipio, the memory of their relationship gives him strength to bear his loss.

88.   **[VII. 23] cumque: cum + –que. Cum** here is a subordinate conjunction introducing a concessive clause. Translate "since" with the subjunctive verb **contineat**.

      Powell prefers a verb in the indicative (**continet**). If one reads the verb in the indicative, then **cum . . . tum** are correlatives and should be translated "not only . . . but especially, in general . . . in particular."

89.   **illa**: refers to **amicitia**.

      nimirum: certainly, doubtlessly, in this respect.

90.   **omnibus**: dative with **praestat**.

      bonam spem: a cognate accusative with **praelucet**; "It (**amicitia**) lights up good hope." (A cognate accusative occurs when an intransitive verb such as **praelucet** takes the accusative of a noun of like meaning.) English would express as "provides good hope." (Powell uses the ablative **bona spe**, a simpler and more direct way to understand the Latin.)

91.   **animos**: accusative subject of the infinitives **debilitari** and **cadere**.

92–93.   Here Laelius stresses the idea that a friend is a second self.

      enim: strengthens **verum**: "but in fact."

      qui = is qui ("he who").

      intuetur < intueor, intueri, intuitus sum: look upon.

      tamquam: as, just as.

93.   **tamquam . . . sui**: translate in this order: **intuetur (eum) tamquam aliquod exemplar sui**.

93.   **quocirca**: therefore, and so.

94–95.   The use of the four connectors here **et . . . et . . . et . . . et . . .** is an example of †POLYSYN-DETON used as a stylistic device to separate each idea so that the reader considers them one at a time, but finally as a whole.

94–96.   **absentes, adsunt; egentes, abundant; imbecilli, valent; mortui, vivunt**: the four pairs of adjectives (used as nouns) and verbs in these phrases display contrasts; i.e., **absentes** is the opposite of **adsunt**, and so on. Cicero uses these opposite pairs to express the idea of the importance of friends: most especially, that the dead are not dead as long as they live on in the minds of living friends.

95.   **dictu**: an ablative supine depending on the comparative adjective **difficilius**; translate **dictu** as "to say."

[VII. 23] Cumque plurimas et maximas com-
moditates amicitia contineat, tum illa nimirum
90   praestat omnibus, quod bonam spem praelucet in posterum nec debilitari animos aut cadere patitur. Verum enim amicum qui intuetur,
tamquam exemplar aliquod intuetur sui. Quocirca
et absentes adsunt et egentes abundant et imbecilli
95   valent, et, quod difficilius dictu est, mortui

Cum

1) worth   (Abl)

2) when

3) since

4) Although (tamen)

Supine

∴ 4th pp in 4th declention
• Ends up like an Adj
• to . . .
• Mirabile dictu. . . . Strange to say

96–98. **tantus . . . laudabilis:** translate in this order: **tantus honos, memoria, desiderium amicorum prosequitur eos, ex quo mors illorum videtur beata, vita horum (videtur) laudabilis.**

96. **tantus:** take as the modifer of **honos** or loosely with the entire series of nouns even though it technically only modifies **honos.**

eos (the friends): take as the object of **prosequitur.**

honos, honoris, m.,: respect, esteem, regard. Note the †ASYNDETON between **honos, memoria, desiderium** in contrast to the †POLYSYNDETON of 93–94.

prosequitur < prosequor: attends upon, is present with, continues with.

97. **amicorum:** "on the part of friends"; subjective genitive depending on the three nouns **honos, memoria, desiderium.**

ex quo: refers to **honos, memoria, desiderium.**

97–98. **illorum** = the former, the departed friends; **horum** = the latter, those left behind.

beata . . . laudabilis: take as adjectives after **videtur.** Cicero continues the thought that a dead friend is blessed because he is remembered and so kept alive by the living friend; the friend who is still alive gets honor for his respect and for mourning for the dead friend.

Here Cicero moves from friendship as a bond between friends to the importance of goodwill and harmony on a larger scale—as the glue that keeps the family and city together. He contends that without cooperation even agriculture would cease to happen.

98. **quod si:** But if.

exemeris < eximo, eximere, exemi, exemptum: take away. The tense is future perfect. English would render as present tense; Latin is very precise about time relationships, indicating with this construction which event happened before another in the future.

99. **rerum natura:** here Cicero enlarges the scale of the argument by referring to society in general.

benevolentiae: goodwill.

coniunctionem < coniunctio, coniunctionis, f.: bond.

100. **ne . . . quidem:** not even.

agri: genitive dependent on **cultus.**

101. **id:** stands for the idea expressed from lines 99–102; "that statement"; i.e., the idea that goodwill is crucial to the well-being of society.

minus: "not" (after **si**); literally, "too little."

101–102. **quanta vis . . . sit:** subjective in an indirect question dependent on **percipi potest.**

103. **percipi < percipio, percipere, percepi, perceptum:** perceive, understand.

vivunt; tantus eos honos, memoria, desiderium prosequitur amicorum, ex quo illorum beata mors videtur, horum vita laudabilis. Quod si exemeris ex
rerum natura benevolentiae coniunctionem, nec
100   domus ulla nec urbs stare poterit; ne agri quidem
cultus permanebit. Id si minus intellegitur, quanta vis amicitiae concordiaeque sit ex dissensioni-
bus atque discordiis percipi potest. Quae enim
domus tam stabilis, quae tam firma civitas est,

105. **quae . . . possit**: subjunctive in a relative clause of characteristic.

      discidiis < discidium, -i, n.: alienation, violent division.

      funditus, adv.: entirely, completely.

106. **quo**: coordinating relative, referring to the ideas expressed in the sentence before; translate "from this."

      quantum . . . sit: subjunctive in an indirect question dependent on **iudicari**.

      boni: partitive genitive dependent on **quantum**; literally, "how much of good." English would render as "how much good."

Points to Ponder:

In line 93 (*Quocirca*) through line 96 (*vivunt*) Cicero uses a series of four opposing ideas that have to do with simultaneous absence and presence of something. List each opposing idea and explain.

Describe the results of removing the *benevolentiae coniunctionem ex rerum natura*.

Explain the concept of a friend as a "second self."

105 quae non odiis atque discidiis funditus possit everti? ex quo quantum boni sit in amicitia iudicari potest.

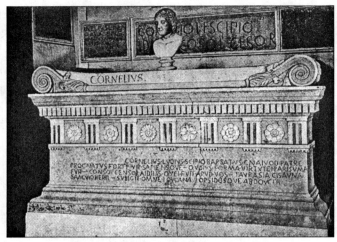

SCIPIO SARCOPHAGUS

SUMMARY OF SECTIONS VII.24–XXVII.100A
OF *DE AMICITIA*

[24–25] Laelius sums up his argument by reiterating that friendship brings together the universe while discord breaks it apart. He intends to bring his discussion to an end, but his two sons-in-law, Fannius and Scaevola, persuade him to speak further, stating that Laelius' friendship with Scipio has given him a knowledge of the subject far superior to any philosopher.

[26–32] Laelius agrees to continue his discussion. He ponders whether friendship exists because men have needs that are met in their friends or whether nature produces friendships because men are attracted to the good qualities that exist in these companions. Laeius decides that it is good character that attracts human beings to one another. He cites such examples from history as Gaius Fabricius, who was loved for his good conduct, and concludes that if we can love men of whom we have only second or third hand knowledge, how much more can we love those with whom we are in contact and who are moral men. He adds that friendship is strengthened by kind acts and increased by intimacy. In answer to his opening question, Laelius says that if friendships were brought about by expediency, then they would dissolve when needs no longer existed; but since nature gives the goodness to men upon which friendships are formed, true friendships will be eternal.

[33–44] In this section Laelius mentions situations that he and Scipio used to discuss concerning friendship. Scipio used to say that it would be very difficult for a friendship between two men to last until the ends of their lives, for in the course of living such things as money, political parties, desire for office, and personal ambitions often separate men from the friends of their youth.

Since this is the case, how far and under what circumstance should a friendship be pursued? For example, should a friend of Tiberius Gracchus have joined him in his battle against the Republic on the reason of friendship alone? Both Laelius and Scipio would affirm that friendship does not demand wrongdoing for the sake of one's friend. The first law of friendship should be that we ask only honorable things of friends.

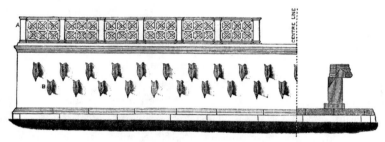

FRONT VIEW OF HALF THE ROSTRA
A. Railing
B. Beaks (Rostra) suspended as trophies

[45–55] Some Greek wise men think that men should avoid close friendships on the basis that they introduce more problems into one's life because the friend's problems are added to one's own problems. Freedom from care should be sought at all costs. Laelius answers that fleeing care is also fleeing moral rightness. It is good character that draws men together; therefore, good men love other good men.

Others think that friendship should be sought for the purpose of protection and assistance; but Laelius argues that it is not the advantage gained that delights, but the love of the friend. Friendships that are based on love alone may also offer utility as a product of the relationship.

Tyrants are those who do not love and are not loved; the result is that they never have those on whose affections they can rely. How foolish, Laelius states, to store up wealth that is here today and gone tomorrow, but to overlook the treasure of friendship that has a permanent value.

[56–66] Laelius next proposes that limitations and boundaries of friendship must be chosen. He states that currently there are three opinions: (1) We should have the same manner of treating a friend that we do in dealing with ourselves; (2) We should treat our friends exactly as they treat us; (3) We should value our friends equally as we value ourselves. Laelius disagrees with all of these opinions. As for the first, he says that we should be willing to do things for our friends that we would not do for ourselves: for example, we would be willing to attack a person who has wronged our friend; but if this same person had attacked us, we might not have reacted. The second view he believes makes the friendship more of an accounting ledger where all accounts must be equal. The third opinion is unjust because one of the friends may have a low opinion of himself, and therefore would feel likewise about his friend.

Since Laelius rejects all of the above opinions, he sets forth his own limits for friendship: (1) When the friends have faultless characters, then they will have complete harmony of opinion in everything. (2) If the friend in some way has a dishonorable intent, then that friend's intent cannot be indulged.

Scipio, as Laelius mentions, used to talk constantly about friendship. Scipio said that men could make better accounts of their sheep and goats than of their friends. Friends should be strong, stable, and constant; but at the outset, it is difficult to tell if potential friends have these qualities; therefore, one should "try out" a potential friend. Since power and politics corrupt, when friends remain constant in the midst of power and politics, they are akin to the gods. The foundation of constancy is faith, for no one is stable who is unfaithful. Laelius reiterates that friendship cannot exist except between good men. Only a good person can uphold these two precepts: a friend cannot be deceitful, and a friend cannot suspect his friend of offense. Friendship should be full of pleasantness, generosity, and sweetness.

[67–73] One should prefer old friends to new ones, thinking of them as being like wines that improve with age, although one should not reject the possibility of a new friend. Friends should treat inferiors as equals, as Scipio did in his circle of friends, but those in inferior positions should not mind being surpassed by their friends.

[74–80] One must not judge a friendship until it has had time to mature. One's childhood friends may not be one's adult friends. Friends should allow for necessary separations. When friends become separated by disagreements, one should be careful in breaking off the friendship; but if the friendship unravels, it should not become a quarrel. One should not begin a friendship too quickly nor choose an unworthy person for a friend.

[81–85] Men who look for profit in friendship deny themselves the enjoyment of a friendship based on love. Each one of us loves himself first and then should look for a friend who is like a second self so that the two become one. It is wrong to expect from a friend more than one is willing to give to that friend. Justice and fairness must be the basis of friendship. Since moral rightness is the highest goal in life, its obtainment can be made easier with the help of a friend. In friendship are found the greatest goals of life: honesty, good reputation, peace, and tranquility.

[86–88] There are many who value not at all goodness, riches, extravagant lifestyles and dinners, honors, or things which most other men admire; but everyone agrees that life without friendship is nothing. Solitude seems to be contrary to nature. Laelius gives the example of a man who is allowed to ascend into heaven and see the universe and the stars. However, when that man returns to earth and finds no friend with whom to share the experience, at that time he finds that such an experience counts for nothing.

[88 contd.–100a] Sometimes friends need advice and admonishment. When these reproofs are given with good intention, they should be well received. The admonishments must lack harshness and insult. If the friend is unable to receive such reproof, then one should regret the friend's moral health. Often when admonished, men become angry over the wrong issue: instead of becoming angry that they have committed a fault, they hate the one who calls the fault to their attention.

The greatest fault is to ignore a friend's faults or worse yet to flatter the friend. Cato said that a person's enemies sometimes do more good than their friends when the former tell the truth and the latter do not. Any pretense in a friendship is a great fault as it destroys the truth upon which friendship must be built. Flatteries only magnify the egos of those who think too much of themselves. Laelius demonstrates the example of this behavior by citing the relationship between the *miles gloriosus* and the sycophant in Roman comedy. While this comic flattery is easy to discern especially by the audience, Laelius warns that in real life flattery can be very subtle and difficult to detect.

In conclusion, Laelius states that his discussion has wandered into more trivial subjects than being a discussion of friendships between wise men of good morals, and he states his intention to return to his first topic and to conclude his discussion.

SELECTION B
LINES 1–63 [SECTIONS XXVII.100B–104]

Laelius is approaching the conclusion of his discussion and addresses his two sons-in-law, C. Fannius and Q. Mucius, as a device to keep the reader focused on the method Cicero has chosen for his thoughts: the young men learning through the life experience of their beloved father-in-law. He builds on his previous topics that friendships can serve as a close bond as long as the friends are morally virtuous men, and that a friend should be one's "second self."

PART 6: LINES 1–37

*Once again Laelius states that friendship depends on moral rightness (**virtus**). He remembers fond relationships shared with his elders and his contemporaries in youth, and now in old age with young men, such as his sons-in-law. Even though Scipio is now dead, he still lives in the heart of Laelius and of others for whom he will serve as an example.*

1. **[100] virtus:** repeated here as a stylistic device to make the point that **virtus** is crucial to Cicero's definition of friendship. **Virtus:** goodness, worthiness, Virtue (personified).

    inquam: defective verb, "I say."

    C. Fanni, Q. Muci: vocatives.

2–3. **in ea:** refers to **virtus**.

3. **convenientia rerum:** harmony of things, complete harmony.

3–4. **stabilitas . . . constantia:** supply *est* with each noun. Note the triple clauses and †ASYN-DETON (lack of connector).

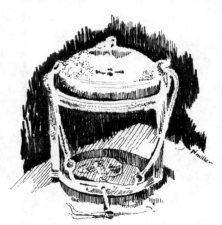

VIRTUS "OSTENDIT LUMEN SUUM."

1   **[100] [XXVII.]** Virtus, virtus, inquam, C. Fanni et
tu, Q. Muci, et conciliat amicitias et conservat. In
ea est enim convenientia rerum, in ea stabilitas, in

4–6.   **quae ... admovet ... -que accipit**: relative clauses having (**virtus**) as their antecedent. The **cum** clauses have as their verbs **extulit et ostendit ... et ... adspexit agnovitque** (Translate as "which, when it has raised itself up and shown forth ... and looked at ... and recognized ..., moves ... and receives ...") Note how elaborate this whole sentence is, as Cicero summarizes the connection between **virtus** and **amicitia**.

4–5.   **cum ... extulit et ostendit ... et ... adspexit agnovitque**: temporal clauses with the indicative.

4.   **extulit < effero, efferre, extuli, elatum**: raise up. Note the CHIASTIC word order in **se extulit et ostendit lumen**.

5.   **idem**: refers to **lumen**.

       adspexit < adspicio.

       id: stands for **lumen**; i.e., the light one finds in another person.

6.   **vicissim**, adv.: in turn.

       illud quod: refers to **lumen**.

7.   **exardescit < exardescere, exarsi, exarsum**: burn, catch fire, burst into flames. Note that this verb continues the imagery suggested by **lumen** earlier in the sentence.

       sive amor sive amicitia: subjects of **exardescit**.

       Note how this carefully constructed sentence (**In ... amicitia**, lines 2–7) that describes the beginning of friendship and affection between individuals mirrors the fact that friendship involves two individuals by using pairs of Latin constructions: (**extulit, ostendit; adspexit, agnovit; admovet, accipit**) culminating in the parallel **sive amor sive amicitia**.

7.   **utrumque**: neuter singular: each (word); refers back to **amor** and **amicitia**.

8.   **dictum est**: Powell prefers **ductum est**, which is a simpler reading; "has been derived (from), is derived from."

       amando: ablative of the gerund. English would put quotation marks around "**amando**" since it represents a word used as a word and not as an idea. Translate literally as "from loving, from the verb to love."

9.   **diligere**: "to like, to feel affection for."

       ames: subjunctive in a relative clause of characteristic.

10.   **indigentia, -ae**, f.: material need, personal need.

       nulla indigentia nulla utilitate: Repetition of **nulla** emphasizes that true friendship is entirely selfless.

       utilitate < utilitas, utilitatis, f.: material gain, personal advantage.

       quaesita: perfect participle passive from **quaero**. Take with **indigentia** and **utilitate** together in an ablative absolute.

       quae: a connecting relative that refers to **indigentia** and **utilitate** together; translate as "and yet this (personal advantage) ... "

ea constantia, quae cum se extulit et ostendit lumen
5   suum et idem adspexit agnovitque in alio, ad id se
admovet vicissimque accipit illud quod in altero est,
ex quo exardescit sive amor sive amicitia. Utrumque
enim dictum est ab amando; amare autem nihil aliud est nisi eum ipsum diligere quem ames,
10   nulla indigentia, nulla utilitate quaesita; quae tamen

11.   **ipsa**: take with **quae** (line 10).

     minus, adv.: translate here as a mild negative, "not quite, not exactly."

11–12.   **si . . . secutus sis**: a future less vivid condition used with the perfect tense (Latin normally uses the present subjunctive here; translate "should pursue." The perfect tense simply indicates that the action is completed before the time of the main verb.)

     secutus sis < sequor.

     eam: refers to the **indigentia** and **utilitate** together ("personal advantage").

12–13.   **[101] hac benevolentia**: ablative of manner; translate "with this sort of affection; goodwill." **Hac nos adulescentes benevolentia senos illos**: note the artful word order here that emphasizes **benevolentia**.

12.   **adulescentes**: take in apposition with **nos**.

13–14.   **L. Paulus** called Macedonicus, the father of Scipio Aemilianus and considered a great general; **M. Cato** one of Cicero's greatest heroes due to Cato's strength of character and gravity (Cicero used Cato as his spokesman in the *de Senectute*); **C. Gallus** known for his literary and scientific learning; **P. Nasica** consul and father of P. Cornelius Scipio Nasica (Serapio) who killed T. Gracchus; **Ti. Gracchus** husband of Scipio Africanus' daughter Cornelia and father of Tiberius and Gaius Gracchus. Cicero, speaking through Laelius, may have chosen to mention them because these men were the role models of his youth.

14.   **Scipionis nostri**: the reader should be reminded that the recent death of Scipio Aemelianus is the motivation for the dialogue of the *de Amicitia*.

15.   **socerum**: take with Gracchum.

     haec refers back to **benevolentia**.

     elucet < eluceo, elucere, eluxi: shines forth, shines out.

16.   **aequales**: men of the same age.

     ut: supply *est*; "as it is."

16–17.   **L. Furius Philus**, **P. Rupilius**, and **Sp. Mummius** were contemporaries and friends of Laelius and Scipio Aemilianus.

17.   **senes**: take in apposition to the subject of **acquiescimus**.

18.   **adulescentium**: genitive plural, dependent on **caritate**.

     acquiescimus: literally, rest in, find comfort in, find pleasure in.

     ut in vestra (caritate): "as in that of the two of you (Scaevola and Fannius)."

19.   **Tuberonis < Q. Tubero** was a nephew of Scipio Aemilianus. Here genitive dependent on an understood *caritate*.

     etiam, adv: even, modifying **admodum**.

19–20.   **admodum**, adv.: modifying **adulescentis**; "quite young."

20.   **P. Rutilii, A. Verginii**: genitives dependent on **familiaritate**.

     Rutilii: P. Rutilius wrote a history of Rome in Greek; he was banished for what was probably a trumped-up charge of extortion and lived in Smyrna where Cicero met him as a young man.

     Verginii: A. Verginius is not known except for this reference.

ipsa efflorescit ex amicitia, etiam si tu eam minus
secutus sis. **[101]** Hac nos adulescentes benevolentia senes illos L. Paulum, M. Catonem, C. Gal-
lum, P. Nasicam, Ti. Gracchum Scipionis nostri
15   socerum, dileximus. Haec etiam magis elucet
inter aequales ut inter me et Scipionem, L. Furium,
P. Rupilium, Sp. Mummium. Vicissim autem senes
in adulescentium caritate acquiescimus, ut in vestra,
ut in Q. Tuberonis: equidem etiam admodum
20   adulescentis P. Rutilii, A. Verginii familiaritate

21–25.   Before the grammatical commentary, we provide a literal translation for this difficult sentence (**Quoniamque . . . pervenire**): "And since the system of (our) life and of our nature has been arranged in such a way that one generation arises (from another), it must indeed be especially desired that you can arrive, as it were, at the finish line with (your) contemporaries, with whom you were let loose from the starting gates."

21.   **Quoniamque: quoniam + –que**: "and since."

   ratio, rationis, f.: rule, law.

   comparata est < comparo, comparare, comparavi, comparatus: arrange, order.

22.   **ut alia aetas oriatur**: result clause dependent on **ita ratio comparata est**.

   aetas, aetatis, f.: generation. Supply *ex alia (aetate)*, as Powell recommends, for this clause to make sense.

23.   **optandum est**: impersonal passive periphrastic; translate literally as "it must be desired"; less literally as "indeed (**quidem**) we must especially hope that . . . "

   ut . . . possis . . . pervenire: a substantive clause dependent on **optandum est**.

23–25.   The idea expressed, that it is most desirable for men of the same age to reach the end of life at the same time, is articulated as a metaphor taken from chariot racing. Contemporaries begin the race of life together just as if they were at a starting gate and should arrive at the finish line at the same time.

   Translate in this order: **Quoniamque ratio vitae naturaeque nostrae ita comparata est ut possis pervenire tamquam ad calcem, ut dicitur, cum isdem aequalibus quibuscum e carceribus emissus sis**.

24.   **carceribus < carcer, carceris,** m.: starting gate.

   tamquam, adv.: as if, just as if.

   tamquam . . . emissus sis: subjunctive in a conditional clause of comparison after **tamquam**.

   emissus sis < emitto, emittere, emisi, emissum, send out.

25.   **īsdem**: ablative plural < **idem**: the same, the very.

   calcem < calx, calcis, f.: finish line.

27.   [102] **caducae < caducus, -a, -um**: frail, transitory, perishable.

   anquirendi sunt < anquiro, anquirere, anquisivi, anquisitum: search (passive periphrastic).

28–29.   **caritate . . . benevolentiaque sublata**: ablative absolutes.

   sublata < tollo.

29–30.   **omnis**: take with **iucunditas**. Note the unusual separation between adjective and noun.

delector. Quoniamque ita ratio comparata est vitae naturaeque nostrae ut alia aetas oriatur, maxime quidem optandum est ut cum aequalibus possis, quibuscum tamquam e carceribus emissus sis, cum isdem ad calcem, ut dicitur, pervenire.

25

[102] Sed quoniam res humanae fragiles caducaeque sunt, semper aliqui anquirendi sunt quos diligamus et a quibus diligamur: caritate enim benevolentiaque sublata omnis est a vita sublata

30–end. Laelius now returns to Scipio with whom he began the dialogue. Laelius articulates that although death has taken Scipio the person away from him, the memories he has of Scipio and their relationship will comfort him. He declares that if he did not have these memories, his grief would be so extreme that he would not care to live. Thus the memory of his friendship sustains him and provides comfort now that Scipio is dead.

30–31. **est . . . ereptus < eripio.**

31. **vivit . . . vivet:** the use of †CHIASMUS here is very powerful, emphasizing the power of friendship and memory.

32. **virtutem . . . amavi:** here and through line 37, Laelius states that he and all posterity will have Scipio's example of moral perfection as a guide.

33. **soli:** dative singular of **solus.**

versatur < versor, versari, versatus est: live, stay. Understand *virtus* as the subject of this verb (i.e., Scipio's virtue or character that has remained with Laelius); **illam** also refers to **virtus; clara** and **insignis** in line 35 modify understood *virtus.*

33–34. **mihi . . . qui . . . habui:** "to me who had." Translate less literally as: "to me . . . , I who had . . ."

34. **in manibus:** idiomatically translated as "within reach."

posteris: dative, parallel with **mihi.**

35. **animo:** courage.

36. **maiora:** neuter plural object of **suscipiet;** it is used substantively as "rather difficult tasks."

36–37. **qui . . . putet:** subjunctive in a relative clause of characteristic.

36. **illius:** refers to Scipio.

37. **proponendam:** set before oneself; supply *esse* as a passive periphrastic construction depending on **putet; memoriam atque imaginem** are the accusative subjects of the infinitive **proponendam (esse).** Translate in the following order: **qui non putet memoriam atque imaginem proponendam (esse).**

POINTS TO PONDER:

In lines 89–91 [VII.23] of the Selection A (*amicitia . . . praelucet*); and in the Selection B, first in line 4 [XXVII.100] ([*virtus*] *. . . ostendit lumen*) and then in line 15 [XXVII. 101]([*benevolentia*] *. . . elucet*), Cicero makes use of light imagery. Examine each of these uses and explain the effect of this figurative language.

As a man ages he has friendships with elders, contemporaries, and finally with those younger than himself. Explain the advantages of each of these situations.

In what way will Scipio serve as an example in the present and in the future?

30 iucunditas. Mihi quidem Scipio, quamquam est subito ereptus, vivit tamen semperque vivet; virtutem enim amavi illius viri quae exstincta non est. Nec mihi soli versatur ante oculos, qui illam semper in manibus habui, sed etiam posteris erit

35 clara et insignis. Nemo unquam animo aut spe maiora suscipiet qui sibi non illius memoriam atque imaginem proponendam putet.

PART 7: LINES 38–63 (THE CONCLUSION)

Laelius delineates all the events shared with Scipio in every public and private activity. His memories of these pursuits make his life still worth living. He concludes by drawing together once more the values of friendship and goodness.

38. **[103] equidem**: an emotional connector introducing a very simple but powerful sentence describing the incomparable value of Scipio's friendship to Laelius.

39–40. **quod . . . possim**: subjunctive in a relative clause of characteristic.

40–43. Laelius lists the three activities he shared with Scipio: political, private, and leisure.

    in hac . . . in hac . . . in eadem: supply *amicitia* in each phrase.

    mihi . . . consensus (fuit): dative of possession. Supply *fuit* as the understood verb for **in hac . . . consensus, in hac . . . consilium**; and finally for **in eadem . . . oblectationis**.

41–42. **rerum privatarum**: take with **consilium** ("advice of/in private matters").

43. **oblectationis < oblectatio, oblectationis**, f.: pleasure, enjoyment.

    illum: refers to Scipio.

43–44. **minima**: take with **re**; ablative of specification (describes that in respect to which something is done. A&G 418) or ablative of cause.

    ne . . . quidem: translated together (not even).

44. **quod . . . senserim**: "as far as . . . I knew." The subjunctive here is in a relative clause of characteristic expressing restriction or proviso.

45. **ipse**: modifies the subject of **audivi**.

    quod nollem: subjunctive in a relative clause of characteristic. **Nihil** is the antecedent of **quod** ("nothing of the sort which . . . ").

46. **isque < is** and **-que**.

    communis: in common; shared.

    idem victus isque communis contains a redundancy used to intensify the idea of **communis**. Cicero means here that Laelius and Scipio were so close that to all intents and purposes they shared the same house, the same taste in food, and the same style of life.

46–48. **neque . . . communes**: read as **neque militia solum (erat), sed etiam peregrinationes rusticationesque (erant) communes**.

47. **peregrinationes < peregrinatio, peregrinationis**, f.: foreign travels.

    rusticationes < rusticatio, rusticationis, f.: country living.

48. **[104] quid . . . dicam**: subjunctive in a deliberative question ("what should I say . . . ").

49. **cognoscendi . . . atque discendi**: gerunds in the genitive case dependent on **studiis**.

    aliquid: object of the gerunds.

    cognoscendi < cognosco: learn, discover.

    discendi < disco: examine.

50. **quibus**: antecedent is **studiis**.

    remoti < removeo: modifies the subject of **contrivimus** (line 51).

[103] Equidem ex omnibus rebus quas mihi aut fortuna aut natura tribuit, nihil habeo quod cum

40   amicitia Scipionis possim comparare. In hac mihi de re publica consensus, in hac rerum privatarum consilium, in eadem requies plena oblectationis fuit. Nunquam illum ne minima quidem re offendi quod quidem senserim; nihil

45   audivi ex eo ipse quod nollem. Una domus erat, idem victus isque communis; neque militia so-lum sed etiam peregrinationes rusticationesque communes. **[104]** Nam quid ego de studiis dicam cognoscendi semper aliquid atque discendi, in

50   quibus remoti ab oculis populi omne otiosum

51.   **contrivimus < contero, conterere, contrivi, contritum**: spend (with **tempus**).

      quarum rerum: coordinating relative that tightly connects the ideas in the sentence before with this one. Additionally by putting this phrase first, Cicero emphasizes how important these shared activities have been to Laelius.

52–54.   **si . . . occidisset, . . . possem**: a mixed contrary to fact condition ("if …had died, I could . . .").

52.   **unā**, adv.: together with, at the same time.

      desiderium, -ii or **-i**, n.: grief; longing for something lost. Latin uses the genitive after this noun; English translates as "for."

53.   **coniunctissimi < coniunctus, -a, -um**: adj., close; closely associated.

      coniunctissimi atque amantissimi: the superlatives placed before the noun they modify (**viri**) make a very strong point about how much Scipio meant to Laelius.

      ferre < fero.

54–55.   **illa**, n. pl.: the subject of three verbs: **exstincta sunt, alunturque et augentur**. Here **illa** refers generally back to **quarum rerum**—all the things Laelius recalls and remembers.

      exstincta sunt < exstinguo: die out, perish. (When **extinguo** is used in the passive as it is here, it has an active meaning.)

      Sed . . . exstincta sunt: translate **nec** as an equivalent to *non*. This first negative clause acts as a contrast to the two positive verbs **aluntur** and **augentur**, which depend on **potius** to make the contrast. Translate this as "But these things have not perished, rather they are both nourished and increased in (my) reflection and my memory."

      potius, adv.: modifying **aluntur** and **augentur**.

56–57.   **si . . . orbatus essem . . . adfert**: the **si** clause is a contrary to fact condition in the past. The main clause uses the indicative instead of the expected subjunctive because it is reporting a fact that is true.

56.   **illis**: ablative with **orbatus essem**. Refers back to **cogitatione et memoria**.

      orbatus essem < orbo, orbare, orbavi, orbatum: deprive of.

      magnum: modifies **solacium**. The distance between this adjective and its noun increases the impact.

57.   **aetas**: old age. Laelius takes comfort from the fact that his advanced age will keep him from living much longer and therefore grieving longer.

57–58.   **diutius . . . iam**: "too long … now."

58.   **in hoc desiderio**: "in this state of longing, grief."

58–59.   **omnia . . . debent**: translate in this order: **omnia brevia debent esse tolerabilia**.

tempus contrivimus? Quarum rerum recordatio et
memoria si una cum illo occidisset, desiderium
coniunctissimi atque amantissimi viri ferre nullo
modo possem. Sed nec illa exstincta sunt
55   alunturque potius et augentur cogitatione et
memoria; et si illis plane orbatus essem, magnum
tamen adfert mihi aetas ipsa solacium, diutius enim
iam in hoc desiderio esse non possum; omnia autem
brevia tolerabilia esse debent, etiam si magna sunt.

60.   **habui**: here has the sense of "I had as my opinion, I understood."

quae dicerem: subjunctive in a relative clause of characteristic expressing restriction or proviso; the meaning is "at least as much as I might say," or less literally, "I had these things to say about friendship."

61.   **locetis** < loco ("value"); subjunctive in an indirect command dependent on **hortor**.

62.   **excepta** < excipio.

ea excepta: ablative absolute; **ea** refers back to **virtutem**.

62–63.   **nihil . . . (esse) praestabilius**: indirect statement dependent on **putetis**.

ut . . . putetis: subjunctive in a result clause dependent on **ita . . . locetis**.

amicitia: ablative of comparison dependent on **praestabilius**.

Cicero concludes the speech by tying together the main themes of **virtus** and **amicitia**.

POINTS TO PONDER:

Describe in detail the life that Scipio and Laelius shared.

How is Laelius able to bear Scipio's loss?

Based on your reading of the essay as a whole, how has Laelius demonstrated that there is nothing more valuable than friendship and that it cannot be obtained without moral worth or goodness (*virtus*)?

60   Haec habui de amicitia quae dicerem. Vos autem hortor ut ita virtutem locetis, sine qua amicitia esse non potest, ut ea excepta nihil amicitia praestabilius putetis.

Figures of Speech

† indicates that these figures of speech are among those required for the Advanced Placement exam.

†ALLITERATION: the repetition of the same letter or sound at the beginning of several words in a series. Example: Sit ita sane; sed eam sapientiam . . . (Selection A, line 10).

†ANAPHORA: the repetition of the same or similar word usually at the beginning of successive phrases. Example: Quoquo te verteris praesto est: nullo loco excluditur: nunquam intempestiva, nunquam molesta est (Selection A, lines 78–80).

†ASYNDETON: the omission of a connector such as "and" or "but" between several words or phrases in a series. Example: Ne id quidem facient negabunt id nisi sapienti posse concedi (SelectionA, lines 18–20).

†CHIASMUS: a reverse arrangement of two phrases so that the second phrase is in an opposite or mirror image to the first phrase. Chiasmus is usually expressed as an ABBA arrangement, named for the Greek letter X (chi). Example: vivit tamen semperque vivet (Selection B, line 31).

†METONYMY: the use of a well-understood quality of something to stand for some aspect or part of the thing. Often in Latin literature, a god is used to stand for the aspect he represents, such as using the name Mars to represent war. Example: Agamus igitur pingui Minerva, ut aiunt (Selection A, lines 20–21).

†POLYSYNDETON: the seeming over-use of connectors such as "and" or "but" between several words or phrases in a series. Example: Quocirca et absentes adsunt et egentes abundant et imbecilli valent . . . (Selection A, lines 93–94).

Bibliography

BOOKS

Everitt, A. *Cicero: The Life and Times of Rome's Greatest Politician*. New York: Random House, 2001.

Konstan, D. *Friendship in the Classical World*. Cambridge: Cambridge University Press, 1997.

Morford, M. *Roman Philosophers*. New York: Routledge, 2002.

Powell, J. G. F., ed. *Cicero the Philosopher: Twelve Papers*. Oxford: Clarendon Press, 1999.

Rawson, E. *Cicero: A Portrait*. Ithaca, NY: Cornell University Press, 1983.

Scullard, H. H. *From the Gracchi to Nero: A History of Rome from 133 BC to AD 68*. Fifth edition. New York: Routledge, 1982.

Wood, N. *Cicero's Social and Political Thought*. Berkeley: University of California Press, 1988.

ARTICLES

Brunt, P. A. "'Amicitia' in the late Roman Republic." In Robin Seager, ed., *The Crisis of the Roman Republic*. Cambridge: Heffer, 1969, 199–218.

Habinek, T. N. "Toward a History of Friendly Advice: the Politics of Candor in Cicero's *De Amicitia*." *Aperion* 23 (1990) 165–85.

Leach, E. W. "Absence and Desire in Cicero's *De Amicitia*." *CW* 87 (1993) 3–20.

Powell, J. G. F. "The Manuscripts and Text of Cicero's *Laelius de Amicitia*." *CQ* 48.2 (1988) 506–518.

Singh, K. L. "On Friendship." In P. MacKendrick, *The Philosophical Books of Cicero*, 213–222. New York: St. Martin's Press, 1989.

Williams, M. F. "Catullus 50 and the Language of Friendship." *Latomus* 47 (1988) 69–73.

COMMENTARIES

Gould, H. E., and J. L. Whiteley. *Cicero de Amicitia*. Macmillan & Co., 1941. Reprint, Wauconda, IL: Bolchazy-Carducci, 2004.

Powell, J. G. F. *Cicero: On Friendship and the Dream of Scipio*. Warminster: Aris and Phillips, 1990.

ADDITIONAL ASSISTANCE

Ancient History Sourcebook: Cicero: Translation of *On Friendship* or *Laelius* at http://www.fordham.edu/halsall/ancient/cicero-friendship.html

Epstein, J. *Friendship: An Exposé*. Boston: Houghton Mifflin, 2006.

Vocabulary

HELP FOR THE VOCABULARY

The following abbreviations have been used in the vocabulary:

abl. = ablative	indef. = indefinite
acc. = accusative	m. = masculine
adj. = adjective	n. = neuter
conj. = conjunction	nom. = nominative
comp. = comparative	pers. = personal
dat. = dative	pl. = plural
f. = feminine	pron. = pronoun
i.e. = that is	prep. = preposition

VOCABULARY

A

a, ab (prep. with abl.), from, away from; by, from, on the part of

absens, absentis, absent

abundo, abundare, abundavi, abundatum, be rich, live in abundance

ac, short for **atque** (conj.), and, and also

accedo, accedere, accessi, accessum, approach

accipio, accipere, accepi, acceptum, accept, receive

acquiesco, acquiescere, acquevi, acquetum, rest in, find comfort in, find pleasure in

ad (prep. with acc.), to, toward, near, up to; in connection, in relation to

adduco, adducere, adduxi, adductum, draw, draw together

adfero, adferre, attuli, allatum, bring

adhuc (adv.), still, yet

admodum (adv.), quite

admoveo, admovere, admovi, admotum, move toward, approach

adspicio, adspicere, adspexi, adspectum, see; look at; behold

adsum, adesse, afui, be present

adulescens, adulescentis, m., young man, youth

adversus, adversa, adversum, adverse

aequales, aequalium, m./f., pl., people of the same age; friends

aeque (adv.), equally

aequitas, aequitatis, f., fairness

aetas, aetatis, f., generation; old age

ager, agri, m., field

agnosco, agnoscere, agnovi, agnitum, recognize

ago, agere, egi, actum, go on, continue on, proceed

aio (defective verb); **ait**, he says; **aiunt**, they say

alienus, -i, m., a stranger; i.e., someone not related to you by birth

aliquis, aliqua, aliquid (pron.), someone, something, anyone, anything; (adj.), some

alius, alia, aliud (adj. and pron.), other, another; **nihil aliud**, nothing other; **alii . . . alii**, some . . . others

alo, alere, alui, altum, nourish

alter, altera, alterum, another

amatus, -a, -um (adj.), loved, beloved, esteemed

amicitia, -ae, f., friendship

amicus, -i, m.,friend

amo, amare, amavi, amatum, love, esteem

an (conj.), whether

angustum, -i, n., narrow limit

animus, -i, m., spirit, soul, mind, heart, courage

anquiro, anquirere, anquisivi, anquisitum, search

ante (prep. with acc.), before; (adv.), before, first, earlier

antepono, anteponere, anteposui, antepositum, place before, prefer

appello, appellare, appellavi, appellatum, call, name

aptus, apta, aptum, fitting, suitable, suited; takes the dat.

aqua, -ae, f., water

atque (ac), (conj.), and, and also

audacia, -ae, f., insolence, daring, audacity

audeo, audere, ausus sum, dare

audio, audire, audivi, auditum, hear

augeo, augere, auxi, auctum, increase

aut (conj.), or

autem (conj.), however, moreover, on the other hand

B

beatus, -a, -um (adj.), happy, blessed

belua, beluae, f., beast; animal

bene (adv.), well

benevolentia,benevolentiae, f., good will, kindness, affection

boni, bonorum, m., pl., good people

bonus, -a, -um (adj.), good

brevis, -e (adj.), brief, short, of brief duration

C

cado, cadere, cecidi, casum, fall, sink

caducus, -a, -um (adj.), frail, transitory, perishable

calx, calcis, f., goal line

carcer, carceris, m., starting gates

careo, carere, —, be without, be free from

caritas, caritatis, f., regard; love, affection

ceterus, -a, -um (adj.), the rest, the other

civis, civis, m., citizen

civitas, civitatis, f., state

clarus, -a, -um (adj.), clear; famous

cogitatio, cogitationis, f., thought, reflection

cognosco, cognoscere, cognovi, cognitum, learn, discover

colo, colere, colui, cultum, honor, revere

commoditas, commoditatis, f., comfort, advantage

communico, communicare, communicavi, communicatum, share, have in common

communis, -e (adj.), common, everyday

comparo, comparare, comparavi, comparatum, join, arrange, put together, order

concedo, concedere, concessi, concessum, allow, grant, concede

concilio, conciliare, conciliavi, conciliatum, make, unite, bring together concordia, -ae, f., concord, unity, harmony

coniunctio, coniunctionis, f., union, connection, relationship

coniunctus, -a, -um (adj.), close, intimate

conquiesco, conquiescere, conquievi, conquietum, rest, repose

consensio, consensionis, f., agreement, harmony, unanimity

consensus, consensus, m., agreement

consequor, consequi, consecutus sum, follow

conservo, conservare, conservavi, conservatum, conserve, preserve

consilium, -ii (or -i), n., advice, plan, design, purpose

constantia, -ae, f., firmness, steadiness, constancy

consuetudo, consuetudinis, f., custom, habit

contentus, -a, -um (adj.), content, happy, satisfied

contero, conterere, contrivi, contritum, with tempus, spend

contineo, continere, continui, contentum, uphold, embrace, sustain, preserve

contraho, contrahere, contraxi, contractum, draw together, unite

conveniens, convenientis, suitable, fitting

convenientia, -ae, f., harmony

corpus, corporis, n., body

cultus, -a, -um, cultivated

cum (conj.), when, since, although

cum (prep. with abl.), with, joined with

cum ... tum (correlatives), in general ... and in particular; both ... and (with the indicative)

cupiditas, cupiditatis, f., longing, desire, passion, lust

D

de (prep. with abl.), about, concerning; from

debeo, debere, debui, debitum, ought, must, owe

debilito, debilitare, debilitavi, debilitatum, weaken, disable

delecto, delectare, delectavi, delectatum, delight, please

denique (adv.), at last, finally

desiderium, -ii (or -i), n., desire, longing for; grief

deus, -i, m., god

dico, dicere, dixi, dictum, say, tell, explain, describe; dictu, to say (after an adj.);

   dictum est, it is said; ut dicitur, as it is said; as people say

difficilis, difficile (adj.), difficult

diligo, diligere, dilexi, dilectum, like, value, love

discidium, -i, n., alienation

disco, discere, didici, examine, learn

discordia, -ae, f., discord, disagreement

dissensio, dissensionis, f., disagreement, dissension, violent division

dissero, dissere, disserui, dissertum, discuss, argue

diutius (comp. adv.), for a longer period of time

divinus, -a, -um, divine, of the gods

divitiae, -arum, f., riches

do, dare, dedi, datum, give

doctus, docti, m., wise man, learned man

dolor, doloris, m., pain, ache

domus, -us, f. (also 2nd declension forms), house, home

dulcis, -e (adj.), sweet, pleasant, delightful

duo, duae, duo (adj.), two

dux, ducis, m., leader

E

e, ex (prep. with abl.), from, out of

effero, efferre, extuli, elatum, raise up

effloresco, efflorescere, efflorescui, blossom, bloom, flourish

egeo, egere, egui, be needy, be in want; **egentes**, needy

ego, mei, mihi, me, me (pers. pron.), I; **egomet** (intensive), I myself

eluceo, elucere, eluxi, to shine forth, shine out

emitto, emittere, emisi, emissum, send out

enim (conj.), for

equidem (adv.), truly, indeed, of course, for my part

eripio, eripere, eripui, ereptum, snatch away, take away

et (conj.), and, even; **et . . . et**, both . . . and

etiam (adv.), even, still, as yet

everto, evertere, everti, eversum, overturn, turn upside down

exardesco, exardescere, exarsi, exarsum, burn, catch fire

excipio, excipere, excepi, exceptum, except, set aside

excludo, excludere, exclusi, exclusum, shut out, exclude

exemplar, exemplaris, n., likeness, copy, image, model

eximo, eximere, exemi, exemptum, take away

expeto, expetere, expetivi, expetitum, desire

exstinguo, exstinguere, exstinxi, exstinctum, destroy; in passive, die out

extremus, -a, -um (adj.), last, final

F

facio, facere, feci, factum, make, do

familiaritas, familiaritatis, f., friendship, intimacy

fere (adv.), for the most part, almost, usually

fero, ferre, tuli, latum, bear, carry

fides, fidei, f., faith, belief, trust

fingo, fingere, finxi, fictus, pretend, invent

firmitas, firmitatis, f., constancy, steadfastness, strength

firmus, -a, -um (adj.), firm, stable, secure

fortasse (adv.), perhaps, probably, possibly

fortuna, -ae, f., fortune, lot

fragilis, -e (adj.), weak, frail, perishable

fructus, -us, m., enjoyment, satisfaction

funditus (adv.), entirely, completely

fungor, fungi, functum, with abl., use, exercise, perform, function, enjoy

G

gaudeo, gaudere, gavisus sum, rejoice

genus, generis, n., type, class, race, family

gero, gerere, gessi, gestum, with **se**, carry on, conduct oneself

gigno, gignere, genui, genitum, give birth to, produce

gravis, -e (adj.), grave, serious

H

habeo, habere, habui, habitum, have, hold, consider, have an opinion, offer

habito, habitare, habitavi, habitatum, live

haud (adv.), not, not at all

hic, haec, hoc (demonstrative pron.), this

homo, hominis, m., man, mankind, the human race, person

honos (honor), honoris, m., honor, distinction, respect, public honor

hortor, hortari, hortatus sum, urge, persuade, advise

humanus, -a, -um (adj.), human

I

iam (adv.), now, already

idem, eadem, idem (pron. & adj.), the same

igitur (conj.), therefore, then, accordingly

ignis, ignis, m., fire

ille, illa, illud (pron. & adj.), that; he, she, it

imago, imaginis, f., image, likeness

imbecillis, -e (adj.) weak

immortalis, -e (adj.), immortal

in (prep. with abl.), in, on; (prep. with acc.) into

incertus, -a, -um (adj.), uncertain

indigentia, -ae, f., material need, personal need

infinitus, -a, -um (adj.), countless, infinite

inquam (defective verb), I say

insignis, -e (adj.), outstanding, remarkable, extraordinary, excellent

integritas, integritatis, f., honesty, integrity

intellego, intellegere, intellexi, intellectum, understand, comprehend

intempestivus, -a, -um (adj.), out of season

inter (prep. with acc.), between, among

interpretor, interpretari, interpretatus sum, explain, interpret, understand, call

intueor, intueri, intuitus sum, look at, look upon

invidiosus, -a, -um (adj.), hated, unacceptable

ipse, ipsa, ipsum (intensive pron.), -self, very

is, ea, id (pron. & adj.), this, that

iste, ista, istud (pron. & adj.), that, that one, that of yours

ita (adv.), so, in such manner

itaque (conj.), and so, therefore

iucunditas, iucunditatis, f., pleasantness, cheerfulness, joy

iudico, iudicare, iudicavi, iudicatum, judge, consider, suppose

iungo, iungere, iunxi, iunctum, join, unite, connect

L

laudabilis, -e (adj.), praiseworthy

laudo, laudare, laudavi, laudatum, praise

levis, -e (adj.), light, easy

liberalitas, liberalitatis, f., generosity, nobility of character

libido, libidinis, f., desire, pleasure, lust

loco, locare, locavi, locutum, value

locus, -i, m., place

loquor, loqui, locutus sum, speak, talk

lumen, luminis, n., light

M

magis (comp. adv.), more

magnificentia, -ae, f., splendor, greatness, magnificence

magnus, -a, -um (adj.), great, large

maior (comp. adj.) < **magnus**, greater

maiores, maiorum, m. pl., ancestors

maneo, manere, mansi, mansum, stay, remain

manus, -us, f., hand

maxime (superlative adv.), very greatly, most greatly

maximus, -a, -um (superlative adj.) <**magnus**, greatest

mediocris, -e (adj.), ordinary

melior, melius (comp. adj.) < **bonus, -a, -um** (adj.), better

memoria, -ae, f., memory

metior, metiri, mensus sum, measure, estimate, value

militia, militiae, f., military service

Minerva, -ae, f., the name of the Roman goddess of wisdom; (by metonymy), wit, head

minimus, -a, -um (superlative adj.) < **parvus**, least

minus (adv.), (after **si**) not quite, not exactly

modo (adv.), just now

modus, -i, m., way, manner

molestus, -a, -um (adj.), troublesome, annoying

mors, mortis, f., death

mortalis, -e (adj.), mortal

mortuus, -a, -um (adj.), dead

multus, -a, -um (adj.), much, (many in pl.)

munus, muneris, n., gift

mutuus, -a, -um (adj.), mutual, reciprocal

N

nam (conj.), for

namque (conj.), for, < **nam**

nascor, nasci, natus sum, be born

natura, naturae, f.,nature

ne . . . quidem (adv.), not even

nec (conj.), (shortened form of **neque**), nor; and . . . not

nego, negare, negavi, negatum, deny, say . . . not

nemo, nullius, no one

neque solum sed etiam, not only but also

neque (conj.), nor; and . . . not

nihil (indeclinable), nothing

nil (indeclinable), nothing

nimirum, without doubt, certainly, to be sure

nisi (conj.), unless, except, if not

nolo, nolle, nolui, not wish, be unwilling

nomen, nominis, n., name

nomino, nominare, nominavi, nomina-tum, name, recall, remember

non (adv.), not, no

norma, -ae, f., a carpenter's square

nos, nostrum (pers. pron.), we (us)

noster, nostra, nostrum, our

nullus, -a, -um (adj.), no, none

numero, numerare, numeravi, numera-tum, number, count

nunc (adv.), now

nunquam (adv.), never

nusquam (adv.), nowhere

O

oblectatio, oblectationis, f., pleasure, enjoyment

obscurus, -a, -um (adj.), incomprehensible, obscure

occido, occidere, occidi, occasum, die, perish

oculus, -i, m., eye

odium, -i, n., hatred, enmity

offendo, offendere, offendi, offensum, offend, annoy, bother

omitto, omittere, omisi, omissum, omit, pass over, pass by

omnino (adv.), altogether, at all (with the negative)

omnis, -e (adj. & substantive), all, every

opportunitas, opportunitatis, f., advantage, convenience, opportunity

opportunus, -a, -um (adj.), fit, suited, appropriate

ops, opis, f., power, wealth, influence

optimus, -a, -um (superlative adj.) < **bonus**, best

opto, optare, optavi, optatum, wish, hope for

orbo, orbare, orbavi, orbatum, with abl., deprive

orior, oriri, ortus sum, rise, rise up, arise

ostendo, ostendere, ostendi, ostentum (ostensum), show

otiosus, -a, -um (adj.), leisure, free

P

pactum, -i, n., agreement; manner; **nullo pacto**, in no manner; not at all

pario, parere, peperi, partum, give birth to, produce, create

partior (and **partio, partire, partivi, partitum**), divide, share

parum (adv.), little, not enough, not sufficiently

patior, pati, passus sum, allow, endure, suffer

pauci, -orum, a few

percipio, percipere, percepi, perceptum, perceive, learn, receive, seize

peregrinatio, peregrinationis, f., foreign travels

peregrinus, -i, m., foreigner, stranger

perfectus, -a, -um (adj.), perfect, faultless

permaneo, permanere, permansi, permansum, remain, stay, abide

perspicio, perspicere, perspexi, perspectum, understand, perceive

pervenio, pervenire, perveni, perventum, arrive

pinguis, -e (adj.), dull, stupid

plane (adv.), entirely

plenus, -a, -um (adj.), full

plurimus, -a, -um (superlative adj.) < **multus**, the most

plus, pluris, n., more

pono, ponere, posui, positum, place, put

populus, populi, m., people

positus, -a, -um (adj.), past participle < **pono**, depending on

possum, posse, potui, can, be able

posteri, -orum, m. pl., posterity, those who come after

posteritas, posteritatis, f., posterity

potentia, -ae, f., power, influence

potiores quam, preferable

potius (comp. adv.), rather

praeclare (adv.), especially well; nobly; very well

praeluceo, praelucere, praeluxi, —, shine, light up

praepono, praeponere, praeposui, praepositum, put before, put ahead, put first, prefer

praestabilis, -e (adj.), excellent, outstanding, superior

praesto (adv.), ready; at hand; present

praesto, praestare, praestiti, praestitum, with dat., excel, stand above

primum (adv.), first, at first

principio (adv.), in the beginning, in the first place

privatus, -a, -um (adj.), private

probo, probare, probavi, probatum, prove, try

prope (adv.), near

propinquitas, propinquitatis, f., kinship, relationship by birth

propinquus, -i, m., a relative, kinsman

propono, proponere, proposui, propositum, put or set forward

prosequor, prosequi, prosecutus sum, follow, accompany, attend upon

prosperus, -a, -um (adj.), fortunate, favorable, prosperous

prosum, prodesse, profui, with dat., benefit, be of benefit

proxime (superlative adv.) <**prope**, nearest

puto, putare, putavi, putatum, think, consider

Q

qua re (adv.), therefore, wherefore, hence

quaero, quaerere, quaesivi, quaesitum, seek, ask

qualis, -e (correlative), such as, as; **talis . . . qualis**, such . . . as

quam (with comp.), than

quamquam (conj.), although

quantum (adv.), as much as, as far as

quantus, -a, -um (adj. & correlative), how much, as much

-que (enclitic), and

queo, quire, quivi (quii), quitum, be able

qui (adv.), archaic abl. used as an adverb, "how"

qui, quae, quod (relative pron.), who, whose, whom, which, that

quia (conj.), because

quid (pron. & adj.), what

quidam, quaedam, quoddam (adj. & pron.), certain

quidem (adv.), certainly, indeed, in fact

quis (pron. & adj.), who

quisquam, quidquam (indef. pron. & adj), any, anyone, anything

quisque, quaeque, quidque (adj. & pron.), each

quocirca (adv.), therefore, and so

quod (conj.), because

quod si (conj.), but if

quoniam (conj.), since

quoquo (adv.), wherever

R

ratio, rationis, f., rule, law

recordatio, recordationis, f., remembrance, recollection

removeo, removere, removi, remotum, remove, withdraw

reperio, reperire, repperi, repertum, find

requies, requietis, f., rest, repose,

res, rei, f., thing, matter, circumstance, situation; res publica, the Republic

reseco, resecare, resecui, resectum, cut back

rusticatio, rusticationis, f., country living

S

sapiens, sapientis (adj.), wise; (noun), a wise person, a philosopher

sapientia, sapientiae, f., wisdom, philosophy

satis (adv. and noun), enough, sufficient

scio, scire, scivi, scitum, know, perceive, understand

secundus, -a, -um (adj.), favorable

sed (conj.), but, however

semper (adv.), always

senex, senis, m., old man

sentio, sentire, sensi, sensum, know, understand

sequor, sequi, secutus sum, follow, pursue

sermo, sermonis, m., speech, conversation

si (conj.), if, if only, if ever, even if

sic (adv.), so, thus

sine (prep. with abl.), without

singuli, -ae, -a (adj.), each one, single

sive (conj.), or seu; or; sive . . . sive, whether . . . or

socer, soceri, m., father-in-law

societas, societatis, f., tie, bond, society, connection

solacium, -ii, n., comfort, solace

solus, -a, -um (adj.), alone, only; neque solum . . . sed etiam, not only but also

specto, spectare, spectavi, spectatum, see, look at

spes, spei, f., hope

splendidus, -a, -um (adj.), splendid, magnificent

stabilis, -e (adj.), stable, firm, secure

stabilitas, stabilitatis, f., stability, security

sto, stare, steti, status, stand

studium, -ii, n., study, pursuit

subito (adv.), suddenly, unexpectedly

sublata, past participle of **tollo**

subtiliter (adv.), precisely, exactly, accurately, in too much detail

sui, sibi, se, se (reflexive pron., never in the nom.), ___self

sum, esse, fui, futurum, be

summus, -a, -um (adj.), highest

superior, superius (comp. adj.), higher, superior, former, above

suscipio, suscipere, suspexi, suspectum, look up to, admire

T

talis, -e (adj.), such

tam (adv.), so; **tam . . . quam**, so . . . as

tamen (adv.), nevertheless, however

tamquam (adv.), as if, just as if, as though

tantum (adv.), only ; so much, as much

tantus, -a, -um (adj.), so much, so great; **tantus . . . quantus**, such (so) . . . as

temeritas, temeritatis, f., whim; caprice; rashness

tolerabilis, -e (adj.), tolerable, able to be endured

tollo, tollere, sustuli, sublatum, take away, destroy

tribuo, tribuere, tribui, tributum, bestow, confer, present, give, allow

tu, tui, tibi, te, te (pers. pron.), you (singular)

tum (adv.), then, at that time

U

ullo pacto, at all

ullus, -a, -um (adj.), any

unā (adv.), together with, at the same time

unquam (umquam) (adv.), ever, at any time

unus, -a, -um (adj.), one

urbs, urbis, f., city

usus, -us, m., use, practice, experience

ut dicitur, as it is said; as people say

ut (conj.), as, since, when; with subjunctive, that, so that, in order that, to

uterque, utraque, utrumque, each, both

utilitas, utilitatis, f., material gain, personal advantage

utor, uti, usus sum, use, enjoy, possess

V

valeo, valere, valui, be strong, be in good health

valetudo, valetudinis, f., health

vel (conj.), or; **vel . . . vel**, either . . . or; (adv.), even

verbum, -i, n., word

vere (adv.), accurately, truthfully

vero (adv.), truly

versor, versari, versatus est, live, stay

verto, vertere, verti, versum, turn

verum (conj.), but, but in truth

verus, -a, -um (adj.), true

vester, vestra, vestrum (possesive adj.), your (pl.)

vicissim (adv.), in turn

victus, -us, m., food; way of life

video, videre, vidi, visum, see; **videor**, seem

vir, -i, m., man

virtus, virtutis, f., virtue, goodness, moral perfection, worthiness

vis, vis, f., force, power, strength

vita, vitae, f., life, experience

vitalis, -e (adj.), vital

vivo, vivere, vixi, victum, live

vivum, -i, n., the quick; the heart

vix (adv.), scarcely, barely

voluptas, voluptatis, f., pleasure; sexual pleasure

vos (pers. pron.), you (pl.)

vulgaris, vulgare (adj.), common, ordinary

CICERO ANCILLARY MATERIALS

CICERO: PRO ARCHIA POETA ORATIO
Student Text by Steven M. Cerutti
Teacher's Guide by Linda A. Fabrizio

Cicero's *Pro Archia Poeta Oratio* is one of the best defenses of literature and the humanities. Cerutti's edition provides a comprehensive treatment of grammatical issues with a keen analysis of the rhetorical devices Cicero wove into the fabric of the oration.

This edition combines the Latin text, running vocabulary and commentary, a brief bibliography, glossary of proper names and places, glossary of terms, and general vocabulary to make it an excellent edition for the AP* and college Latin classroom.

The new *Pro Archia Poeta Oratio Teacher's Guide* by Linda A. Fabrizio is designed to meet the needs of the busy AP* teacher. It includes the oration in large print suitable for photocopying, a literal translation of the oration, a select bibliography, and a set of assessments/questions with sample answers.

Student Text: xxviii + 132 pp (2006) Paperback 6" x 9" ISBN 978-0-86516-642-4

Teacher's Guide: (2006) Paperback 6" x 9" ISBN 978-0-86516-616-5

*AP is a registered trademark of the College Entrance Examination Board, which was not involved in the production of, and does not endorse, this product.

 BOLCHAZY-CARDUCCI PUBLISHERS, INC.
WWW.BOLCHAZY.COM

CICERO ANCILLARY MATERIALS

DRAMATIC READING OF THE ENTIRE *Pro Archia* IN RESTORED CLASSICAL PRONUNCIATION.

THE LIVING VOICE OF LATIN
Cicero: Selections
Read by Robert P. Sonkowsky

Cicero Selections: *In Catilinam* I (complete), *Pro Archia* (complete), selections from other speeches of Cicero, from his rhetorical and philosophical treatises, and from his poetry.

Booklet and 2 cassettes, Order #23680

O TEMPORA, O MORES: A BRIEF *Vita* OF CICERO.

CICERO THE PATRIOT
Rose Williams

Light-hearted in tone but faithful to the facts, this volume interweaves Cicero's private life and feelings with the development of his public life and literary output. Supplementary materials make this an invaluable resource for both students and teachers.

Features: • Complete description of events and historical circumstances of Cicero's life • Timeline of events and publication of Cicero's works • Glossary of terms • One-page summary of Cicero's life

Teacher's Manual Features: • Suggestions for study enrichment • Sample report topics • Further information for the teacher • Thought questions for students • Quick questions to test comprehension

Student Text: vi + 92 pp. (2004) Paperback 6″ x 9″
ISBN 978-0-86516-587-8

Teacher's Manual: xi + 74 pp. (2004) Paperback 6″ x 9″
ISBN 978-0-86516-588-5

 BOLCHAZY-CARDUCCI PUBLISHERS, INC.
WWW.BOLCHAZY.COM

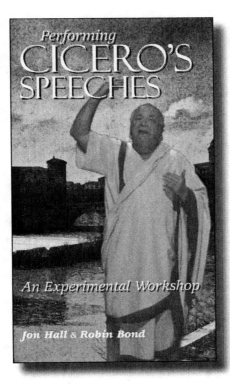

THE LOCK

Cicero—he stood alone against Rome's tyrants!

Benita Kane Jaro

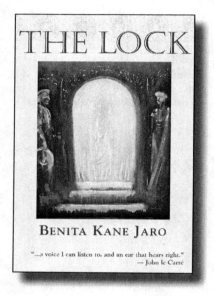

The Lock, though it is a completely independent novel, continues the portrait of the collapsing Roman society of the late Republic so brilliantly depicted in The Key. The principal figures of the age—poets, scholars, soldiers, politicians, powerful political women, even slaves, Julius Caesar, Cicero, Pompey the Great—all make their appearance and play out their fateful struggle.

Benita Kane Jaro is an exciting writer of great skill and grace. Courage, too...The result is a powerful and moving story, as freshly minted as today's news and as haunting as the deepest memory.

–George Garrett

If there is to be a worthy successor to Mary Renault, or to Marguerite Yourcenar, it may be Benita Kane Jaro.

–Doris Grumbach

xxii + 282 pp, original illustrations (2002) Paperback ISBN 978-0-86516-535-9

BOLCHAZY-CARDUCCI PUBLISHERS, INC.
WWW.BOLCHAZY.COM